To Tony,
Thanks for your
Inspiration &
Leadership,

Martine

Praise for *Inside the Minds*

"Unlike any other business books, *Inside the Minds* captures the essence, the deep-down thinking processes, of people who make things happen." - Martin Cooper, CEO, Arraycomm

"What C-Level executives read to keep their edge and make pivotal business decisions. Timeless classics for indispensable knowledge." - Richard Costello, Manager-Corporate Marketing Communication, General Electric (NYSE: GE)

"Want to know what the real leaders are thinking about now? It's in here." - Carl Ledbetter, SVP & CTO, Novell, Inc.

"A snapshot of everything you need to know..." - Larry Weber, Founder, Weber Shandwick

"True insight from the doers in the industry, as opposed to the critics on the sideline." - Steve Hanson, CEO, On Semiconductor (NASDAQ: ONNN)

"Unique insights into the way the experts think and the lessons they've learned from experience." - MT Rainey, Co-CEO, Young & Rubicam/Rainey Kelly Campbell Roalfe

"Unlike any other business book." - Bruce Keller, Partner, Debevoise & Plimpton

"The *Inside the Minds* series is a valuable probe into the thought, perspectives, and techniques of accomplished professionals. By taking a 50,000 foot view, the authors place their endeavors in a context rarely gleaned from text books or treatise." - Chuck Birenbaum, Partner, Thelen Reid & Priest

"A must read for anyone in the industry." - Dr. Chuck Lucier, Chief Growth Officer, Booz-Allen & Hamilton

"An incredible resource of information to help you develop outside-the-box..." - Rich Jernstedt, CEO, Golin/Harris International

www.Aspatore.com

Aspatore Books is the largest and most exclusive publisher of C-Level executives (CEO, CFO, CTO, CMO, Partner) from the world's most respected companies and law firms. Aspatore annually publishes a select group of C-Level executives from the Global 1,000, top 250 law firms (Partners & Chairs), and other leading companies of all sizes. C-Level Business Intelligence ™, as conceptualized and developed by Aspatore Books, provides professionals of all levels with proven business intelligence from industry insiders – direct and unfiltered insight from those who know it best – as opposed to third-party accounts offered by unknown authors and analysts. Aspatore Books is committed to publishing an innovative line of business and legal books, those which lay forth principles and offer insights that when employed, can have a direct financial impact on the reader's business objectives, whatever they may be. In essence, Aspatore publishes critical tools – need-to-read as opposed to nice-to-read books – for all business professionals.

Inside the Minds

The critically acclaimed *Inside the Minds* series provides readers of all levels with proven business intelligence from C-Level executives (CEO, CFO, CTO, CMO, Partner) from the world's most respected companies. Each chapter is comparable to a white paper or essay and is a future-oriented look at where an industry/profession/topic is heading and the most important issues for future success. Each author has been carefully chosen through an exhaustive selection process by the *Inside the Minds* editorial board to write a chapter for this book. *Inside the Minds* was conceived in order to give readers actual insights into the leading minds of business executives worldwide. Because so few books or other publications are actually written by executives in industry, *Inside the Minds* presents an unprecedented look at various industries and professions never before available.

INSIDE THE MINDS

Inside the Minds:
The Pharmaceutical Industry

Leading CEOs on Developing Niches, Differentiating Products and the Future of Specialty Pharma

BOOK IDEA SUBMISSIONS

If you are a C-Level executive or senior lawyer interested in submitting a book idea or manuscript to the Aspatore editorial board, please email jason@aspatore.com. Aspatore is especially looking for highly specific book ideas that would have a direct financial impact on behalf of a reader. Completed books can range from 20 to 2,000 pages – the topic and "need to read" aspect of the material are most important, not the length. Include your book idea, biography, and any additional pertinent information.

Published by Aspatore, Inc.

For corrections, company/title updates, comments or any other inquiries please email info@aspatore.com.

First Printing, 2004
10 9 8 7 6 5 4 3 2 1

Copyright © 2004 by Aspatore Books, Inc. All rights reserved. Printed in the United States of America. No part of this publication may be reproduced or distributed in any form or by any means, or stored in a database or retrieval system, except as permitted under Sections 107 or 108 of the United States Copyright Act, without prior written permission of the publisher.

ISBN 1-58762-046-4 Library of Congress Control Number: 2004108649

Inside the Minds Managing Editor, Carolyn Murphy, Edited by Michaela Falls, Proofread by Eddie Fournier, Cover design by Scott Rattray & Ian Mazie

Material in this book is for educational purposes only. This book is sold with the understanding that neither the authors nor the publisher are engaged in rendering medical, legal, accounting, investment, or any other professional service. For legal advice, please consult your personal lawyer.

This book is printed on acid free paper.

A special thanks to all the individuals who made this book possible.

The views expressed by the individuals in this book (or the individuals on the cover) do not necessarily reflect the views shared by the companies they are employed by (or the companies mentioned in this book). The employment status and affiliations of authors with the companies referenced are subject to change.

Inside the Minds:
The Pharmaceutical Industry

Leading CEOs on Developing Niches, Differentiating Products and the Future of Specialty Pharma

CONTENTS

Dr. Martine Rothblatt   7
ETHICAL BIOTECHNOLOGY

Richard B. Hollis   21
A VISION TO CREATE GLOBAL
PHARMACEUTICALS

Gregory J. Mossinghoff   37
AN INSIDER'S VIEW OF THE PHARMACEUTICAL
INDUSTRY

Dr. Anthony H. Wild   51
THE EMERGING POSITION OF SPECIALTY
PHARMACEUTICAL FIRMS

Dr. Cameron Durrant   71
DO ONE THING REALLY WELL: FINDING A
NICHE IN SPECIALTY PHARMA

Ethical Biotechnology

Dr. Martine Rothblatt

Chairman and CEO
United Therapeutics

A Unique Approach

Our company creates medicine for chronic, life-threatening conditions and then makes the medicines available to the physician/patient community for those illnesses. One big difference between my company and other companies in the industry is that we don't operate our own laboratories but instead form partnerships with university biochemistry departments and life sciences departments, and agree to fund research at those universities that is likely, in our opinion, to result in a commercialized medicine. We also supplement that approach by buying other companies that have taken the medicine-development process to a certain point, but are really not capable of conducting the final studies necessary to get regulatory approval and to market their drugs. So, in the first place we form a partnership with universities, and in the second case, we use the merger and acquisition process to acquire promising biotechnology companies.

The largest benefit of partnering with universities is that it's much more cost-effective because we're able to piggyback on the infrastructure that a large university creates for life science research. If we were to do it differently, we would need to build ourselves a biochemistry building and laboratories, purchase all the expensive equipment that fills the laboratories, and add to our payroll all of the scientists and research doctors who are already employed at universities. Ours is a much more cost-effective approach.

The Three Golden Rules

The Golden Rules for the pharmaceutical industry are the same Golden Rules for doctors, because pharmaceutical companies are really like corporate doctors, or composite doctors, or organizational doctors. The first rule for doctors should be the first rule for pharmaceutical companies: do no harm. Don't test harmful drugs on patients or do things that will cause harm, such as create demand for a drug (for example, airing too many TV commercials) where the demand doesn't inherently exist.

The second golden rule for doctors is the same as the second golden rule for pharmaceutical companies: try to do good. Try to cure a disease, don't try to maintain a person in the diseased state so that you can keep selling them medicine. That means that pharmaceutical companies have the obligation to always continue to do research to develop better and more improved medicine, even if it means that those new medicines may take away business from some of their existing medicines. In the end a healthier, longer-living population is the best customer for the pharmaceutical industry.

Finally, the third most important thing for doctors and the third most important goal for the pharmaceutical industry is to respect the autonomy of the patient. Doctors need to involve patients in decision-making, and pharmaceutical companies also need to involve patients in decision-making. Right now the information included with a drug that you purchase from the pharmacy is all but indecipherable by a typical patient. Or, what you see printed on the back of the ad in a magazine in micro small font — let's be realistic, what kind of person is really going to understand all of that? I think the pharmaceutical industries have an obligation to present information in a way that a common person of ordinary intelligence can understand the pros versus cons of taking that particular medicine.

In summary, the three Golden Rules: do no harm, try to heal the patient, and respect the autonomy of the patient.

A Successful Product

A successful product moves through three stages of a process. First, it must become a potential medicine; something that has a reason to work as a medicine. The middle stage of the process is to prove scientifically that the product in fact can treat the illness successfully. The third part of the process is persuading patients and physicians that this is a medicine they want to use, because many times there are multiple medicines for the same illness.

The most important factor is the doctor interest, but nowadays many doctors pay increasing attention to patients' wishes, and that's the result of growing bioethical recognition of individual autonomy. Prominent television advertising of medicines has been quite negative. It has created a mindset of people perceiving that the society is surrounded by more disease than it is. It has created a disease gestalt among society. I, for one, would prefer that that kind of medical advertisement be sharply curtailed.

The first factor that makes a product sell is that it's safe. The second most important factor in selling is that it's effective. The amount of testing is really proportional to the number of people who are likely to use a product. I think a good, rough rule of thumb is something will be tested on one-tenth of one percent of the estimated maximum amount of people that it's likely to end up being used on. For example, if the maximum number of people that may use something is one million people, then it should be tested on at least 1,000 people.

One disease that we focus on is called pulmonary arterial hypertension (PAH). We focus on this disease with our drug Remodulin. Our clinical studies have proven the usefulness of Remodulin for PAH, and it was approved by the FDA. We spend a lot of energy making Remodulin available to doctors and patients. We like to make Remodulin available to doctors who want to do more studies with it, to make it commercially available to patients who want to purchase it through their insurance, and to continue doing research to improve Remodulin, based on the feedback that we hear from our doctors and patients.

Product Development, Case in Point

In developing a game plan for Remodulin, we started off looking at the current situation at the beginning of the business plan. That involved how many patients were suffering from this illness, what medications were being used to treat this illness, and how much money was being spent on these other medicines. We then realized that, although a lot of money was being spent on other medicines, they weren't satisfying the needs of the doctors or the patients — the side effects were too bad. We decided to look for a medicine that would treat these patients and doctors with many fewer side effects. That laid the groundwork.

We then calculated that if we were able to replace the current medicine in this field, it would pay for all the costs associated with getting regulatory approval for Remodulin. We developed a business case and showed that it had a positive net present value, meaning that the present value of the profits — selling Remodulin at an appropriate estimated discount rate — were greater than the present value of the costs involved in developing Remodulin. (This was based on the inherent time value of money.) With that positive net present value for the project, we decided to invest the money and succeed in the market.

A Personal Marketing Approach

I found the most effective marketing strategies are one-on-one meetings with doctors, especially in a group setting where one doctor who has had positive results with your drug can then share his experience with other doctors who have not used your drug. I think that is the single most effective way to market your drug, because doctors will believe other doctors sooner than they'll believe the drug company.

Patents

Patents are very important to drug companies because they give you some assurance that after you've gone through all the trouble of getting your drug approved, somebody won't come along and eat your lunch, so to speak. We keep patent lawyers on retainer all the time and have them meet every three months with our scientists to learn what new ideas the scientists have thought up and to write them up and file patents on the best ideas.

Challenges in the Pharmaceutical Industry

The biggest challenge that our company faces in the current marketplace is proving that drugs work to the very exacting standards required by the FDA, and that probably is every company's biggest challenge. The FDA has a standard that says they will approve a drug only if in two separate studies the chance of the drug working only by chance — in other words that it was a placebo effect, that you thought you were taking something that would help you and you actually got better — is only 5 percent. So, let's suppose you conduct a big drug study comparing your drug to a placebo, and the people taking your drug get better, which would ordinarily be the case. Also, typically, some people taking the placebo get better, because some diseases fade away on their own. When the statistics are finished, the chances of your drug being effective due to the placebo turns out to be 7 percent. Chances are the drug works if there is only a 7 percent chance of the drug being effective due to placebo effect. However, the FDA won't approve the drug because their very hard and fast rule is 5 percent. This is an arbitrary, out of the blue number, but it is one that statisticians long ago proposed and the FDA accepted.

That's the biggest challenge facing drug companies: to successfully meet this standard in light of countless vagaries involved in conducting clinical studies of medicine. Those vagaries include that there are many genetic tendencies in people that we are only scarcely aware of, that different medical centers will conduct a study in slightly different ways, that some drugs have different effects if a person takes them in the morning or at night, on a full stomach or an empty stomach, that we can't really control all these aspects of peoples' lives.

In a study you try to get an even match of men and women, of placebo and active groups of different genetic backgrounds; you try to do a good job of teaching all the different centers to administer the drug in the same way, to take the measurements in a standardized fashion. You try to have as large a study as is realistically possible, because in a larger study the chance of random error becomes smaller and smaller — those errors tend to average out. But, if you make your study too big, you'll never find enough patients to fill it or it'll take too long to find enough patients to fill it and, by the time you get your drug approved, other drugs may have been approved that compete with it.

In spite of all these uncertainties, to prove that something still works with a chance of luck being only 5 out of 100, is a very demanding challenge. What we do is we try to hire the best experts we can find in clinical development, and they in turn try to design a study that has as small a chance of confounding factors as possible. Nobody is omniscient and it's never really possible to reduce the element of risk to zero. There are many, many times that a company conducts a drug study and one time the chance of the results being due to error is 3 percent, which means, "Wow, the drug really works, we'll be approved." The next time they do the study, the chance of the results being due to error is 10 percent. You would think that the drug still works, but the FDA won't approve it because *both* studies have to be less than 5 percent chance of error.

Risks in the Pharmaceutical Industry

The biggest risk is that the clinical trial won't be successful. What you do is take a look at smaller studies — studies of ten or twenty people — and you look at the theory and try to understand logically why the drug should work, and then you ask yourself, "Did it work when it was tried on just a few people?" You make the best guess that you can. I would say that it's analogous to drilling wells for oil in that you take a look at the theory, which would be like the geology of the rock formations, and people say, "Well, based on our knowledge of these rock formations, there should be oil in this place." And then you drill some test wells to see if there actually is oil in this place. Then, you make a huge investment and hope you get a gusher. As, most people know, the theory can be right and you still can't get any oil out of a test well. And sometimes everything is going in your favor and then unforeseen factors mess you up, like the country goes to war. So, the closest industry that I'm aware of to drug development is drilling for oil.

Another big risk is competition. There are over 500 biotech companies and thousands of academic researchers looking for cures. Many times a competitor develops a better medicine. In that case, all of your investment may be unrecoverable.

Public Misconceptions

I think the biggest misconception that the public has about the pharmaceutical industry is that they can *reliably* and *readily* produce safe and effective cures for diseases. About 99 percent of what a pharmaceutical company produces turns out to be worthless. There is approximately only one in every hundred potential medicines that a pharmaceutical company works with that actually ends up being safe and effective. The public probably knows that not every medicine is going to be approved, but they might think that one out of every five or one out of every ten would be. We know less about the human body than we know about the nature of our galaxy. We know less about the lifetime of a number of our cells than we know about the lifetime of other galaxies billions of light years away. We are incredibly ignorant about the complex interactions of the human body. So, while we can somewhat deceive ourselves that our theories explain to us exactly what should and should not work, for every hundred molecules developed pursuant to that theory, 99 percent don't work at all.

In regard to getting closer to understanding the human body, I would say that we aren't materially so. There is a lot of hype in the newspapers that because we have decoded the human genome we should be much closer to developing cures. But the biggest shock to people when the human genome was decoded was that it was only about two-thirds larger than the genome of a worm. These were the people who were the great experts; the great experts who, up until just a few months before the genes were decoded, did not realize that the human genome is hardly more complicated than the worm genome. The human genome ascribes a much vaster array of proteins to be made and hence, there's a new field of proteomics. The human genome is really like an alphabet and to say that understanding the human genome will tell you how to cure disease is sort of like saying that knowing the alphabet will tell you how to write a novel. It just doesn't work that way. It's only a starting point. That's why a lot of herbal remedies do work because for hundreds, thousands of years, people have seen that everybody who eats this particular berry got better of such and such a problem.

Our greatest selling medicines are by and large simply pure, standardized forms of herbal remedies that have been around for hundreds of thousands of years. Aspirin, for example, is a standardized, pure form of the bark of a tree, which was known to people in Europe for many hundreds of years as a pain reliever. That's the case with many, if not actually most, of our modern drugs. So, I think we are a long way away from really understanding how to treat diseases. We have had some successes, but we've also had some failures. We've been successful in treating some viral diseases, especially HIV. On the other hand, new viral diseases have appeared, such as SARS, that we didn't even realize were coming. In fact, it's estimated that there are approximately one million different types of bacteria in the world, and we've categorized only about 100,000 of them. We don't know what 90 percent of the bacteria in the world are or how they exist. It's a similar situation with viruses. We don't know what 95 percent of the viruses are, and they are constantly mutating. The fact of the matter is that when it comes to medicine, the only thing we really know is how much we don't know.

Changes in the Pharmaceutical Industry

A huge change was the development of health insurance, because health insurance provided people with a way to buy as much of a drug as they needed regardless of how much money they had. As a result, it allows people to buy a lot of drugs that they really don't need, because it's not coming out of their pocket. It's a very odd industry in that the person who is the primary customer for a pharmaceutical company is the doctor, because he is the one who writes the prescriptions that order the product, but the doctor doesn't pay for it. So, you have people ordering products who have no real concern or care for what the product costs. The end person using it, if he's insured, is not paying for it except indirectly perhaps through an increase in his premium.

For the majority of people the health insurance premiums are paid by their companies. Medical insurance really created an immense cash cow from which the pharmaceutical industry is able to milk its udders to fund the development of new and exciting medicines. I'd say health insurance was the biggest boon for the pharmaceutical industry. If the pharmaceutical industry was really smart, instead of fighting Medicare reimbursements for pharmaceuticals, they should support it. Because right now the only people who have to pay out of their pockets for pharmaceuticals are older people who don't have any insurance other than Medicare, and those people who routinely use much less of a pharmaceutical because they simply can't afford it.

Another change is the focus on wellness in healthcare. This has given rise to the concept of prophylactic medicines, if you will, which in turn has morphed into a huge business of nutriceuticals; people are taking nutritional supplements with the goal of improving their health even though there's nothing actually wrong.

Keeping Up With Changes in the Industry

To keep up with changes in this industry, it is most important for professionals to go to the medical conferences. Doctors attend these disease-specific conferences to share their growing knowledge base each year. Industry representatives can also attend the conferences, where they can listen to the scientists and doctors share their knowledge about the diseases, or read the published papers from the proceedings.

For patients to keep up with changes, they need to be involved in patient organizations, which exist for most diseases, and attend meetings of the patient associations to see which needs are not being met. Patients can then give feedback to the pharmaceutical company for improving the medicine to meet their needs better. Customer service is very important to us, but I don't think we'd use that phrase. We'd use a phrase like "medical affairs" or "patient affairs." What it really means is letting the patients and doctors know that we care about their opinions and concerns, we're listening, and when we take a request to get back to them, we do, and we close the loop and tell them how we've addressed their concerns.

The Future of the Industry

The electronic technology is going to have a huge impact, and people don't really see it coming right now. Medical sensors will become good enough, coupled with high-speed Internet lines, that the process of going to a doctor will become more and more rare. Instead, people will have more of their medical checkups done in the privacy of their own homes.

Medical knowledge will become increasingly computerized so that an artificial, intelligence-based doctor will be smarter and more capable of diagnosing a condition than any human doctor can be. If you think about it, when human doctors diagnose a condition, they are just going down a logic chart saying, "Well, a person has a temperature and a sore throat, so it must be this, this, or that." They run blood tests, eliminate a number of things, and arrive at a specific diagnosis. That's exactly what computers are best at—logic trees. I think that in the future, more and more prescriptions will be generated by computer intelligence, and the healthcare field will have to adapt itself to accept computer-generated prescriptions from a computer system, which has been certified by the health insurance industry as being as competent as a doctor.

I'd like to see the industry take greater responsibility for the rest of the world. Right now in the pharmaceutical industry, the only markets that receive attention and focus are the US, Europe, Canada, and Japan. Very little attention is being paid to South America, Africa, or Asia. I think the pharmaceutical industry would find it in its interest to actively create and enable affordable health insurance mechanisms in the developing countries, and then to begin to make their medicines available in the developing countries. After all, four-fifths of the world's population is in those countries, and they're 99 percent ignored by pharmaceutical companies. I do what I do to try to help people and to try to make the world a better place by making it a healthier place. I think our industry as a whole is doing the same.

Martine A. Rothblatt, Ph.D., J.D., M.B.A. started United Therapeutics in 1996 and has served as Chairman and Chief Executive Officer since its inception. During the 1980s, Dr. Rothblatt co-founded the international satellite communications operator PanAmSat and later launched the nationwide satellite-based vehicle tracking industry. In the early 1990s, Dr. Rothblatt created the digital satellite radio broadcasting industry by obtaining the necessary regulatory approvals and by starting the companies that are currently providing this service in the US and overseas. In 1995, she endowed the PPH Cure Foundation which subsequently merged into the William Harvey Medical Research Foundation, a charitable organization that she continues to serve as President.

Acknowledgement – Robyn Barst, M.D., James Crow, Ph.D., Paul Mahon, Esq., Fred Hadeed, Roger Jeffs, Ph.D., Robert Daye and Teresa Bongartz

A Vision to Create Global Pharmaceuticals

Richard B. Hollis
Founder, Chairman & CEO
Hollis-Eden Pharmaceuticals, Inc.

Endeavoring to develop drugs to treat and cure human diseases is a daunting but noble pursuit that requires a clear and firm vision. Even with the significant advances made in medicine, there are many diseases and disorders still to treat and newly emerging threats to tackle. It is a long and winding road to success with multiple obstacles that must be overcome along the way.

First and foremost of these of course is the time and expense involved in successfully bringing a new drug to market. For any one drug, pharmaceutical and biotech companies have to go through a rigorous regulatory process, which can take anywhere from ten to fifteen years. It is intense and costly, requiring anywhere from $200 million to $800 million to take a drug from discovery through development and commercialization.

To succeed in this process requires a broad array of specialties and disciplines that include drug research and development, clinical and FDA regulatory processes, and ultimately manufacturing and marketing a product to the healthcare community. The keys are to be strategic in choosing the right drug to put through the regulatory process, knowing how your drug works and having the ability to design human clinical trials and protocols that will generate sufficient data to establish safety and efficacy in the FDA regulatory process.

It is difficult to be successful, because to get through that ten or fifteen-year development cycle, you have to have enough staying power and access to capital to get your drug to the marketplace. A lot of biotech companies prematurely license their technology to big pharmaceuticals, selling it at a discount compared to its potential commercial value because they cannot afford to take the drug to market themselves. Our vision at Hollis-Eden is to become a self-sustaining, revenue-generating entity that does research and development in the pharmaceutical industry for decades to come. While we anticipate that Hollis-Eden will choose to partner some of its compounds for large market indications that would benefit from the leverage of a larger sales force or development team, we will do so selectively and only at a time when we have advanced the value of those compounds as far as we can on our own.

Getting Started in the Industry

When starting a pharmaceutical company, you not only have to have a good idea of the diseases you want to target, you must also have a new or better approach for the way in which to treat the disease. Our approach at Hollis-Eden is to specialize in a category of hormones found in the human body that have been implicated in the majority of immune system-related diseases. The hormones we are working on have been written about in the scientific and medical literature for decades, but their potential role and benefit in treating human disease was not fully understood or articulated, and were overlooked as therapeutic development candidates as a result. The purpose for starting Hollis-Eden was to further investigate the potential role these hormones could play in the body and then to develop and commercialize them as therapeutic medicines – what we call Immune Regulating Hormones – for the benefit of patients. What we have found is that these hormones play a central role in regulating immune and metabolic functions. Unfortunately, these hormones are known to be depleted as we age, and this process can be accelerated as a result of infectious diseases and other chronic immune system disorders. Hollis-Eden's approach is to re-design these hormones as pharmaceuticals to simulate or regulate the body's immune system to potentially control progression of a number of different diseases and conditions.

With the vision of developing a drug for global use, I founded Hollis-Eden in 1993 with a drug called HE2000, or IMMUNITIN ™, for global infectious diseases such as HIV. I wanted the product to be safe and effective, but practical so that it could be accessible to all countries irrespective of their world status. The way I looked at it, if you were flying 100,000 feet above Earth, what would you see as the biggest problem facing the world today? It would have to be global infectious disease pandemics. HIV is a good example and actually it is in the beginning stages of the epidemic. We are up to 45 million infected today, and it is projected that in the next five to ten years that number will jump to 90 million. When you go to the developing world, it is devastating because HIV is taking out a whole generation of human beings who are supposed to be the workforce and provide an economic structure, and that is all going to be lost. The problem is the current treatments for HIV, although beneficial to some, are not practical enough to truly benefit the masses due to the relatively sophisticated infrastructure needed to implement them and the ability of the virus to evade the current antiviral drugs.

That is why we initially set out to target HIV with our immune regulating approach. When someone is infected with HIV and progresses to full-blown AIDS they often die from opportunistic infections because their immune system cannot mount a response. In 1994, we began doing the development work to prepare one of these hormones to put into human beings. We did that until 1997, and in 1998 we started human clinical trials in HIV. Through this process we have measured a lot of immune cells, and our biggest discovery was the fact that these particular hormones can re-regulate a dysregulated immune system and restore its ability to respond more optimally to HIV. The interesting thing about that is that it had been speculated in the literature that these hormones were associated with aging. They were called the anti-aging hormones. It has been said that HIV is advanced aging of the immune system. So if you could re-regulate the immune system, then our HIV research has implications in several diseases where immune dysregulation is a factor. In addition to the epidemic of HIV, malaria infects 300 to 500 million people a year and one third of the world has tuberculosis. A healthy immune system can more or less deal with TB and malaria, but when the immune system becomes compromised with HIV, you have the susceptibility to co-infections and those people are really vulnerable to opportunistic infections such as tuberculosis.

A Global Agenda

Earlier in my career, I believed that the world was not paying enough attention to these diseases, and the drugs that were available at the time were going to run their course, and pathogens would mutate and develop resistance to their effectiveness. Someone had to look at designing a drug that would not create resistance, would be cost-effective and could be used for multiple diseases. Today we are developing IMMUNITIN to treat these infectious diseases, primarily HIV, malaria and tuberculosis. My vision for IMMUNITIN was an immune-based product that was not targeting the pathogen but instead targeted the immune system. These hormones would send a signal to the immune system and balance the response to the pathogen. This was a totally different approach. Rather than using chemotherapy and trying to poison a pathogen, we would use hormones to signal the immune system to keep the pathogen in check or to eliminate it.

When I founded Hollis-Eden, I recognized the enormous need and opportunity to serve humanity by developing compounds that could have a global impact on infectious diseases. The company still has that vision, and the need remains. While drugs have been approved for HIV, they are very expensive. Because they cost $10,000 to $20,000 in first-world countries, they cannot be used in the developing world. The current estimates are that, even with the resources being made internationally to purchase and distribute these drugs in developing countries, only 3 million of the 42 million who are infected with HIV are likely to be treated over the next few years.

Considerable progress has been made in focusing and strengthening the resolve of the world community to address the growing threat of global infectious diseases. Everyone concerned about the devastating toll of global infectious disease should welcome the progress being made towards removing one of the key stumbling blocks to winning this war – providing sufficient financial resources to begin seriously tackling the pandemic. At the same time, however, it should also be of concern that the focus to date appears to be predominately on funding distribution of currently available drugs rather than on new drug research and development. While currently available drugs may bring benefit to many HIV sufferers in the short term, more needs to be done to incentivize development of next-generation therapies better suited for the challenges inherent in fighting a global war on HIV. Such therapies should be economically sustainable, non-toxic, easy to use and not lead to drug resistant strains of the virus.

Unfortunately, incentives to develop new drugs appropriate for global markets do not exist. In fact, the current structure creates a strong disincentive to develop such drugs because the message that has been loudly sent is that patents on drugs for HIV, malaria and TB should be ignored and countries in need should feel free to buy generic copies. This raises the question of how a biotechnology or pharmaceutical company can justify ever investing in the development of a drug that is designed for use in these countries, when even if it is successful it is likely to be "nationalized."

A novel approach by the U.S. government to spur development of new drugs to counteract bioterrorism may provide a useful model for incentivizing development of new therapies for global infectious diseases. Called Project BioShield, the $6 billion, ten-year initiative encourages industry to develop new drugs that will address the clear shortcomings of existing therapies and guarantee that industry will be appropriately rewarded for developing important new medical countermeasures to weapons of mass destruction. Following the BioShield model, one possible approach would be to have a portion of globally available funds set aside to encourage the development of new drugs. With those funds, developers could be guaranteed that if they successfully develop a new infectious disease drug that is practical for global use and are willing to make it available to an organization such as the World Health Organization for distribution at manufacturing cost, then they would receive a significant annual licensing fee that could be earned as a profit. This would then address the intellectual property issue, because non-profit agencies could manufacture the new drug for the cheapest possible price, and there would be an incentive for health organizations to amortize the fixed annual license fee over as many doses as possible—thus maximizing the number of patients treated. In my opinion, this should be the goal of any program in this area.

Building a Broad Product Pipeline

In addition to IMMUNITIN and our global vision for infectious disease, we also have developed additional product candidates based on our Immune Regulating Hormone technology. Among these, we have a compound called HE2100, or NEUMUNE ™. We are developing that drug with the United States government as an anti-radiation drug. When a person is exposed to radiation, it destroys the body's infection-fighting cells generated in the bone marrow. NEUMUNE stimulates the reproduction of those cells in the bone marrow that are killed off by the radiation. The drug is designed to be used in the case of a nuclear emergency, not only by military personnel that may encounter nuclear weapons on the battlefield but also emergency responders, healthcare workers and civilians that my be exposed to lethal doses of radiation from an act of terrorism.

A third drug, HE2200, or REVERSIONEX ™, is, as of this date, in a Phase II human clinical trial where the drug is being used in patients over 65 years of age in combination with a hepatitis B vaccine. In this trial, we are studying the drug's ability to stimulate an elderly person's immune system enough that they produce more protective hepatitis B antibodies than those patients receiving the hepatitis B vaccine alone. If we can do that and allow them to respond much better to the vaccine, it establishes the premise that we can reverse immune incompetence in the elderly. I think that has big implications in medicine.

Because we are measuring a lot of human immune system responses in our human clinical trials, we are learning that our immune regulating hormones are able to stimulate a variety of cells in the body that are dysregulated as a result of the disease conditions. For example, we know we can reduce inflammation, which is an over-responsive immune response. We made that discovery when we were studying HIV patients receiving IMMUNITIN as a single therapy.

That has big implications, because in autoimmune disorders the underlying problem is an over-reactive immune response; the immune system is basically attacking itself. If we can target these hormones for specific disorders and lower those inflammatory markers, we potentially can be very effective in treating these diseases, of which there are more than 80, including diabetes and rheumatoid arthritis.

The Business Plan

In building a pharmaceutical company, it is not enough to have a deep and extensive pipeline–eventually you have to get those drugs to market to generate revenue and earnings. As a smaller, innovative biotech company competing against larger pharmaceutical companies, you have a big decision to make at the Phase II stage. Are the data robust enough that Wall Street will respond and give you access to capital, which you can use to conduct the Phase III clinical trials yourself and commercialize that product? Or is it more advantageous to form a strategic partnership with a large pharmaceutical company?

We've decided to take NEUMUNE for the indication of radiation protection all the way through commercialization ourselves. For some of our other products we may decide to partner with a larger pharmaceutical company, because the Phase III trials in some indications are extensive, and drugs in some areas of medical treatment require massive marketing resources. A large pharmaceutical company may have a much broader distribution and sales force network that is already addressing a particular disease indication.

With IMMUNITIN, we decided that before we move into Phase III clinical trials, we would try to form global partnerships to develop the drug so we can price it cost effectively around the world for developing countries, but still retain our patents and the ability to make a reasonable profit. It is a global public health issue when you start talking about diseases like HIV, malaria and tuberculosis in developing countries where there are hundreds of millions of people infected with those diseases. We have talked to the World Health Organization and heads of government in developing countries, and we are trying to figure out how we can develop it at a sustainable price.

We are poised to be a later-stage development company, moving from the early-stage research and development to the later-stage development and commercialization. We can potentially file for FDA approval for NEUMUNE by late 2004. We would then count on that drug to start generating revenues for the company so we can become self-sustaining.

Our company has been able to establish a strong patent portfolio with these hormones that gives us the commercial right to develop them as pharmaceuticals. We are positioned nicely for the long term because we have been able to target our pharmaceuticals to multiple diseases, and we have strong patents that allow us to justify spending investor money to get these products to the marketplace. We have also been able to shorten our discovery time because we have the compounds, and we are reducing the development cycle because we have a good understanding of how they work. That could get us to the marketplace much quicker than the ten to fifteen-year timeframe. We may even be able to get our drugs to the market in just five to seven years.

The Values Behind the Plan

In my opinion, to be effective any business plan needs to be formulated on the foundation of a solid set of principals and values that guide the company over the years. Communicated to stakeholders both within and outside the company, these principals and values provide the roadmap and compass that keep the company on course regardless of the challenges and hurdles that might arise. At Hollis-Eden, I have given a great deal of thought to our guiding operating philosophies, principals and values, and strive to keep them top of mind among all of our employees as we pursue the execution of our plan. One of the first documents the company produced in the early days was a statement of philosophy and you will find it on our website as well as in our investor kits as an integral part of our company description.

The Challenges Ahead

In drug development there are numerous hurdles that can potentially stand in the way of success. Among these of course is the complex regulatory process. However, we now have an FDA commissioner who is not only an M.D., but also a Ph.D. in economics. He can appreciate the scientific, medical and economic sides of drug development. The FDA is always going to be a hurdle because drug development is so highly regulated. But I think that is good, because the regulatory process is trying to protect the consumer. The key is to fully understand your drugs so you make it easier on yourself to get over the regulatory hurdle.

Another challenge is to make sure patents are defensible. If you have a successful drug, it is going to draw a lot of commercial interest and competition. Your patents are going to have to be able to withstand that scrutiny. Also, we are moving into a tough time with issues of reimbursement and the cost of drugs. A big concern is whether you can manufacture and develop these drugs and still price them so they can be competitive in the industry and still make a reasonable profit. If you are unable to recoup your drug development costs, you will not be able to justify moving forward with that drug. You have to have significant profits to draw investor interest, and enough revenues and profits so that you can keep funding research and development. Without money to invest in future drugs, your revenues are eventually going to dry up and you are not going to be attractive to investors.

One of the things that is really hurting the industry is the perception that pharmaceutical companies are overpricing their drugs. That is an unfair stigma because it is very expensive to develop a drug. Moving into the 21st century, the pharmaceutical industry is going to have to do a much better job of educating consumers about the cost effectiveness of our technology and the role we are playing in treating diseases. Healthcare is a huge industry with lots of costs and a large infrastructure, and drugs are just one component. The drug companies are often targeted for criticism because of the perceived high costs of their products. In reality, pharmaceuticals that treat and cure diseases are cost effective because they create less dependency on the healthcare system, but the public at large has the wrong perspective because we have not done a good enough job positioning the industry.

At the national level, two major crises facing our society are the threat of emerging new strains of infectious diseases, and bioterrorism. We do not talk too much about infectious diseases here in the United States, because we think we have most of them under control with antibiotics, but the problem is that our drugs are facing resistance and losing effectiveness. We overuse antibiotics, and soon there are going to be strains of pathogens that are resistant to antibiotics. We are going to have to take a hard look at what to do when that happens.

One of the biggest challenges both here in the U.S. and in the world at large is the instability of world affairs in regards to terrorism. Today there are eighteen countries with access to nuclear material, and there is more instability in the Middle East than ever before. I feel weapons of mass destruction on our soil and around the world represent the biggest threat to the human race, because if one of those WMD hits us, we are in big trouble. That is why we are working with our military on an anti-radiation drug. If we are not prepared for an eventual outcome like that, can you imagine what could happen? It would create unprecedented panic and hysteria. A lot of pharmaceutical companies have not woken up to this new market potential yet, but I believe our industry is going to be critical to the whole anti-terrorism effort.

Project BioShield is new legislation to stimulate the private sector to create the next generation of pharmaceuticals to deal with WMD. I believe Hollis-Eden is going to be one of the pioneers leading the way. If we do not develop these medical countermeasures, where will we be in this era of bioterrorism? The pharmaceutical industry needs to wake up to the fact that it is a whole new world, and we will be called upon to deliver these next-generation countermeasures to WMD. If we do not develop this technology, America is not going to be prepared for what many people call an inevitable outcome.

The Future of the U.S. Healthcare Industry

As a nation, we're going to have to start finding answers to the very expensive healthcare system in the United States. If there is not economic incentive in the healthcare system, it is not going to stimulate innovation.

People talk a lot about the Canadian system, where everyone is insured. That sounds great, but that system does not provide the quality of healthcare that our system provides. What we have proven is that the private sector always provides better quality and more innovative technology. However, the system we have now with Medicaid and Medicare, combined with the private sector, is beginning to be too costly.

The answers are not straightforward. If you look at the limitations of universal healthcare and the strengths and limitations of our system, you start to realize that the best way to get the answer is to keep healthcare in the private sector and have some government involvement in getting greater access to healthcare without squashing innovation. There is no way that 40 million Americans should not be insured, but there is also no way that we should decrease the quality of our system.

That said, I do not believe you can have a totally egalitarian healthcare system. If certain people can afford better healthcare because they have the financial resources, they should be able to do that. It is a dilemma that has been around for ages, but in the next five, ten or fifteen years, it will be the major issue.

The other big move in healthcare is going to be more and more preventive medicine – staying healthy longer. How can you keep the aged healthier and out of the hospital? How do you keep them from being a drain on the healthcare system? Since we have a "gray wave" coming– that population that is moving into their 60s and 70s – someone has to figure out how we are going to cover all those people. Drugs and technologies that prevent further complications and disease progression will be essential in keeping healthcare costs for the elderly down.

In general, I'd like to see the pharmaceutical industry promote a better image in terms of how it is improving the quality of life for millions of people around the world. We need to show that we cure and prevent diseases and that our fair and reasonable profits justify the enormous costs to develop a drug. I would like to see a healthcare system that honors our patents; a healthcare system that can provide greater access for all without compromising the innovation and creativity that results

A VISION TO CREATE GLOBAL PHARMACEUTICALS

from a free marketplace. If you don't have these visions, you should ask yourself why you are in this business.

Richard B. Hollis founded Hollis-Eden Pharmaceuticals in August 1994. Mr. Hollis currently serves as Chairman, President and Chief Executive Officer. Mr. Hollis has over 25 years experience in the healthcare industry in a variety of senior management positions. Prior to founding Hollis-Eden, Mr. Hollis served as Chief Operating Officer of Bioject Medical from 1991 to 1994 and as Vice President Marketing and Sales/General Manager for Instromedix from 1989 to 1991. From 1986 to 1989, Mr. Hollis served as a general manager of the Western business unit of Genentech, Inc., a manufacturer of biopharmaceuticals. Prior to joining Genentech, Inc., Mr. Hollis served as a divisional manager of Imed Corporation, Inc., a manufacturer of drug delivery systems. Mr. Hollis began his career in the healthcare industry with Baxter Travenol. Mr. Hollis received his B.A. in Psychology from San Francisco State University.

An Insider's View of the Pharmaceutical Industry

Gregory J. Mossinghoff
President
Inspire Pharmaceuticals, Inc.

Industry Background

In the last 50 years breakthrough treatments discovered and developed by the pharmaceutical industry have brought about dramatic increases in longevity. Whether viewed from the perspective of large, established pharmaceutical companies or small biotechnology startups, there is no better area to work in today. People in this industry have the talent, capability and opportunity to make a real difference in patients' lives by pioneering new approaches to diseases with real unmet medical need. The ability of the industry to provide these important advances to humankind, combined with an interesting and challenging career pathway for motivated individuals and the strong potential for profitability, makes the pharmaceutical industry one of the most attractive all-round fields of endeavor today. Because it is a highly complex and regulated industry, mastering every facet is difficult for any individual. This presents a challenge, but also a lifetime opportunity for any highly talented and driven person. It also creates a situation in which teamwork is essential for success and is itself a differentiating factor between success and failure. Talent and culture are both, therefore, important to achievement.

No matter the size of a company, there are certain basic similarities among innovative pharmaceutical companies. We are all developing proprietary drugs for the prescription pharmaceutical market. Most often, companies have patent protection or some kind of exclusivity that prevents other companies from developing and marketing the same product. But that protection only lasts for a limited time. That life span is very definite and very real. When that period ends, any number of generic pharmaceutical companies can produce generic versions of the original innovative product. This is great for patients in that eventually innovative products become economically priced, but it means that innovative companies must continuously develop new products in order to survive and thrive over the long term.

Innovation and creativity are critical to bring forward new treatments. Quite literally, this is a life and death struggle, a fact which is starkly evident in small companies. We do see a number of biotech companies every year, for example, that do not make it and end up being sold or liquidated. A list of the top ten companies twenty years ago would look very different from today's list. This is not necessarily true in other industries. Consumer products companies like Procter & Gamble and Gillette have brands with no real end to their life span – Tylenol™, Crest™ toothpaste, Gillette™ razor blades, etc. This is not so in the pharmaceutical industry. No matter how successful a particular prescription product is, eventually it will go generic or over-the-counter. That's a similarity all innovative pharmaceutical companies share, whether they are large or small.

By contrast, one important difference between large and small companies is that the larger competitors have a critical mass due to the great number of products in their pipelines and a higher quantity of marketed products. It is therefore less a daily struggle for existence and more a continuous drive for new products, and it is generally easier for large companies to produce enough new ideas in order to generate new products to keep their pipelines full. Small companies that are dependent on only a few products face the death of the company if they are not successful in stocking their pipelines. The level of risk they face compared to a large company is dramatically different. Big companies can survive a drop in their industry standing, and even in their stock without going out of business given their vast resources. The smaller companies often cannot afford such a dramatic setback in their research and development activities.

Of course, in some cases, a big company that is weak over a long period of time is at risk of a takeover. Merger and acquisition activity is always on the mind of leading pharmaceutical executives. The industry has seen a great deal of consolidation over the last five to ten years for this reason, and the pace of major consolidation will probably continue given the declining rate of generation of truly new, innovative products. A number of large players have been created by consolidation—Glaxo-SmithKline, Astra-Zeneca, Pfizer (now a conglomeration of a number of small companies, including Pharmacia) and Bristol Myers-Squibb. However, the leading companies are now so large that to become much larger may not necessarily lead to better research and development productivity. Ultimately, it's all about productivity, growth and what pharmaceutical companies, large and small can bring to the marketplace. With more growth comes the increased challenge of managing a larger company and increasing sales, so it appears that continued consolidation might not serve the large companies or the industry well in the foreseeable future.

Major Misconceptions about the Industry

Because the pharmaceutical market in the US is to a large extent a free market, it is important that the industry continuously demonstrate that new products introduced into the marketplace demonstrate clear value for money. For example, many new chronic-use medications are priced in the neighborhood of $3.00 a day, generally speaking the price of one daily meal. So the product really must make a difference in patients' everyday daily lives in order to justify this pricing level. The product must make it possible for the patient to do things that otherwise would not be possible or easy, such as read, watch TV, exercise or any number of activities of daily living. If the alternative to the new product is to live with a debilitating disease, which is essentially ruining the patient's ability to easily conduct his or her life, then the product is certainly worth $3.00 a day, if not much more.

It takes a tremendous investment in time and resources, in the face of very long odds, to move a new product through the R&D process and onto the market. A company needs to be passionate about working through a number of hurdles over many years, and working closely with the FDA to get a product on the market. When it finally is launched, people need to see the intrinsic value relative to the cost. Unfortunately, there is a serious misconception out there—that drugs should essentially be free. Perhaps this is because it is possible to buy generic aspirin for mere pennies per tablet. New products not only need to be priced to recoup the cost of goods, but more importantly the R&D investment, time and risk that it took to develop the product. If a patient perceives that the product is not providing appropriate value for the money, then the patient shouldn't buy it or the managed care organization should not reimburse it. However, if the product is useful and provides tangible benefit to a patient's activities of everyday living and/or quality of life, the payer, whomever that may be, should not expect it to be free, or close to it. As pharmaceutical companies, we have to make a profit in a sustained, long-term way. And the way we do that is simply to provide value for money and price accordingly.

Creating a Niche

From the perspective of a small company, a niche market can be an advantage. Inspire was founded and first funded in 1995 based on technology licensed from the University of North Carolina having to do with mucosal surface health and defense mechanisms. The mucosal surfaces are those exposed, directly or indirectly, to the outside environment. This would include, for example, the nasal passages, the upper respiratory tract, the eyes, mouth, throat, lungs—everything except the skin. The concept is to activate receptors on these mucosal surfaces by applying the drug topically, whether it's inhaled, intranasal, a topical eye drop or a nasal spray. When those receptors are activated, defense mechanisms kick into gear and cleanse those surfaces of particles, pathogens, antigens and allergens, leading to better surface health. Specific diseases resulting from a deficiency in the mucosal surface include dry eye, allergic rhinitis and cystic fibrosis. Our proprietary compounds have been targeted to address those diseases and others with a number of programs now in clinical development.

Research & Development

Discovery and clinical development are the two general areas of research and development. Our processes are based on the tried and true methods of medicinal chemistry. We create synthesized molecules, which are variations of the original technology platform set of molecules, and we test those molecules through a number of different techniques to determine their potency, receptor affinity and so on. Once we have a molecule that we think is potent, has an affinity for the receptor and is likely to be tolerated, we test it in the discovery phase to make sure it's safe for animals first and ultimately for people.

There is a battery of animal tests that need to be done. We test for toxicology, pharmacology (to see if the drugs are active) and side effects. Once a compound has been synthesized, scaled up, all the tests have been completed and a large amount of the compound has been made, if it looks like it should go to clinical testing, then we file an Investigational New Drug (IND) application with the FDA. The company will typically meet with the FDA to discuss the product and to get its approval to move into human testing.

Clinical Development

The next step is clinical development, which has three distinct phases. Phase I is essentially to test the safety of the compound. Phase I trials normally take place in healthy volunteers and on a small scale, with up to several hundred patients.

If the drug is found to be safe, we move into Phase II, which is limited to testing on humans who have the actual disease we are addressing. In this phase we are focusing on safety again, but we're also looking for clinical pharmacology—that the product is actually doing what we want it to do. So this is a critical stage of development in the overall process.

Once we have determined in Phase II that the compound is safe and does what we want it to do in a relatively small number of patients, we can move into Phase III, which we call pivotal testing. Here we run large, well-controlled pivotal trials in several thousand patients in anywhere from two to several trials. The idea in this phase is to make sure that the drug is safe on a broader scale and to prove statistically the efficacy of the drug. To get FDA approval of a new drug, it generally takes two well-controlled pivotal trials showing a statistical difference with the drug compared to a placebo. If that is accomplished, all the data can be put together in a New Drug Application (NDA) and filed with the FDA.

The company then waits its allotted time according to the FDA schedule. At the end of this period, there are three possible outcomes: 1) the product is approved for commercial use subject to all of the FDA-required labeling and documentation for patients and practitioners; 2) the product is approvable, in which case the FDA may ask for more information; or 3) the product is not approvable. Under the Prescription

Drug User Fee Act, there is a specific schedule under which the FDA must provide a concrete response to the application in exchange for the industry paying fees whenever an application is filed.

Taking the Product to Market

From the time when we first have a compound that we believe will work, it takes a couple of years before we can file an IND and begin human testing. Human trials usually take about four or five years if they go reasonably quickly. Then the NDA can be filed with FDA, and approval generally takes about a year to eighteen months. Altogether it's about ten years before we can actually start selling the product. Patents, which grant the company twenty years of exclusivity, are filed in the early discovery stage, so by the time we get a product to market it may have only ten or so years of patent protection remaining.

Educating physicians, patients, pharmacists and other healthcare professionals is the name of the game in gaining acceptance for the new drug in the marketplace. The education process is restricted by the FDA, which has guidelines for promotional materials. Those materials contain the features and benefits of the product and must be approved by the FDA. In addition, the industry polices itself with its own code of ethics and behavior about what can and cannot be said and done in promoting the product.

A number of sales representatives, marketing professionals, brand and sales managers all coordinate the effort of developing key messages about the product. The sales representatives take the promotional materials out into the field, set up appointments with physicians and other healthcare practitioners and meet with those people to talk about the product and how it could benefit particular patients. It's a commercial sale just like any other sale. The difference is that the features and benefits of each product in a particular therapeutic category are presented to the healthcare professional in order to influence prescribing activities, and at every point along the way what can and cannot be said about the product is clearly defined.

This is very much a relationship business. Most prescriptions written for new and existing products are a result of relationships between sales representatives and physicians based on a high level of product education. That is supplemented with journal advertising, and to some extent, television and other major media advertising. There is much more advertising for prescription pharmaceutical products than there was ten years ago, which is a major change in the landscape. But the primary business driver is still prescriptions written for a particular brand based on the relationship between the representative and physician.

The Effects of Increased Advertising and Public Information

Feedback, surveys and market research tell us that the effect of increased promotion and availability of information to the public is generally positive. Patients today are much more informed than they have ever been, and they research products on their own. Because of the strong influences of television advertising and other media, they proactively ask their physicians about particular brands. When a patient asks a physician for a specific brand by name, if the product is appropriate to address that patient's need, the result is a prescription written for that product. Physicians are generally positive about direct-to-consumer advertising because they can have a more intelligent conversation with those informed patients than they otherwise would.

Insurance companies and other payers may see an increased demand for these products. For example, millions of Americans are now taking cholesterol-lowering drugs, and this has no doubt led to decreased mortality from chronic heart disease, helping patients and providing the healthcare systems involved significant savings. Even though payers have been pushing back on direct-to-consumer advertising, the fact that they have to pay for these products is positive from the perspective of improved overall patient health.

What Makes a Successful Product?

A product that effectively treats a reasonably large portion of the patients who are known to have a particular disease is considered a successful product. We have a fairly sophisticated understanding of epidemiology for any given disease; for example, we know with good accuracy how many people get the disease annually or how many people have the disease at any given time.

Generally speaking, each therapeutic area has competing products. There are very few areas that have no prescription product on the market. Any time a company can take a reasonable market share away from competing products because their drug offers superior features and benefits—it can be taken fewer times per day, or it has fewer side effects, etc.—the company should be able to gain a certain amount of market share. If that can be done, it's a successful product.

The key to success is innovation -- coming up with ideas, taking those ideas and applying them, and doing it rapidly and efficiently under very extensive regulations. When a company does that well and consistently, the company will no doubt be successful. The critical point is that the pharmaceutical business is a risky one, yet it can be highly rewarding. But most importantly, the industry develops treatments that will help people live better lives.

Recent Industry Trends and Changes

The amount of information that goes into the average New Drug Application has dramatically increased over the past generation. This is due in part to FDA requirements, and also in part to the fact that companies have bigger budgets and can do more testing of compounds. The result has been an increase in complexity, size and cost of the average application to market a new drug. That's a trend that will hopefully slow or reverse in the future, so that the pace of development and launch of novel treatments can accelerate to the benefit of patients and the pharmaceutical companies that employ thousands of talented, creative people. One cannot talk about the industry without mentioning the pressures on the pricing of new products exerted by the payers. Virtually every European country, as well as Canada and Japan, has a single payer system, so these countries have enormous leverage on pricing as the ones buying the drugs. In the U.S., however, we still have a free market consisting of multiple payers and multiple sellers. This creates a more efficient market from the industry perspective. We can set our price as necessary and appropriate in order to recoup the research and development investment we have made in the product.

In comparison, countries outside the US are not as concerned about the long-term health and viability of the pharmaceutical companies. They are more concerned with ensuring that the cost is as low as possible because they have limited resources to spend on health care. Bargains are being driven so hard and prices so low that R&D is leaving some of those single-payer countries. As a result, biotech is suffering in these countries as well, because if a company develops a product and cannot achieve fair pricing that will ensure that the company recoups its investment and stays viable, it is simply not worth the effort. These are businesses, after all, not charitable organizations.

For this reason the biotechnology industry is faltering in Germany and France, and even in the U.K. That is the reason we see a thriving biotech industry in the U.S. and other countries that have more liberal pricing behavior. However, there is a decline in others. Glaxo-SmithKline, arguably a U.K. company, has most of their R&D operations in the U.S. The same is true of Astra-Zeneca, another U.K. organization that does most of its R&D in the U.S. A. Lots of R&D dollars are being spent in the U.S. now because of the free market on pricing. Should the US decide for short-term expediency to change this, the long-term viability of the pharmaceutical and biotechnology industries would be in serious jeopardy.

It is very important to note that it is actually possible to kill the industry. For example, in Canada about a generation ago, they invoked so-called compulsory licensing, where after a very short time all new products were required to be licensed to generic companies. Essentially the industry left the country and today very little, if any, real R&D is being conducted in Canada. This is the reason prices are low in Canada and the US pharmaceutical industry is faced with the issue of parallel importation.

Commissioner Mark McClelland of the FDA has done an exceptionally good job of framing the argument as to why all countries should pay their fair share of the cost of innovation if they want to see breakthrough medications launched. His point is essentially that it shouldn't be a situation where everyone is a free rider on the backs of the U.S. consumer, but that is what has happened, especially in Europe. The Europeans have to understand that it is not only fundamentally unfair but also bad business to drive to the lowest possible drug price in the short-term because they will ultimately drive the industry off their continent. And if Europe doesn't support a big pharmaceutical industry, it is really not possible to sustain a biotech industry either, because one is dependent on the other. Those countries would end up with no innovation in life science. Commissioner McClelland has taken a persuasive argument directly to these other countries. Hopefully that argument will succeed in bringing about needed change on the pricing front.

In summary, the key issues facing the industry are consolidation, research productivity, and the amount of information required by the FDA and pricing pressures. Looking at the stock prices of the big U.S. pharmaceutical players over the past couple of years, one can see all of these forces reflected in relatively low stock prices. The U.S. leads the world in biotech, pharmaceuticals and the number of new drugs produced, and we have a net export of these products. It's an incredibly important component of many communities and states to have a viable pharmaceutical industry, and hopefully these critical issues will be faced and resolved so that we will see the long-term survival of one of America's true success stories and the envy of the world.

The Future of the Industry

It has been said that the pharmaceutical industry is like an oyster. When some kind of irritant, sand or grit gets inside the oyster, it creates a pearl around that foreign body. And that is traditionally what the industry has done. Any time there has been a major issue, the industry has managed it wisely. And it has turned out to be a pearl. In that respect, it's an industry that is very resilient due to its abundance of talented people and dedication to the noble cause of fighting disease.

Still, focused effort will be needed to overcome these aforementioned challenges. A more level playing field in terms of global pricing and a general global agreement about levels of profitability would be a wise course. The minute we say as a global community that we do not need innovative medications is the minute we stagnate. We are saying that there is no need to seek better, longer lives. The vast majority of us do not want that as a goal. As long as the desired goal is improved health, having new and innovative medications, and therefore a vibrant pharmaceutical and biotechnology industry, is a vital component to achieving this vision.

Mr. Mossinghoff is President of Inspire, and also serves as a member of the Board of Directors and as the company's Secretary. He joined the company in 1998. Since that time, he has been responsible for overseeing all business-related activities, including business development, finance, strategic planning and commercial operations. Since joining the company, Mr. Mossinghoff has coordinated Inspire's public and private financings, including representing the company in its IPO, its six major corporate partnership agreements and various academic license agreements. He has over fifteen years of experience in the pharmaceutical industry. Prior to joining Inspire, Mr. Mossinghoff was worldwide Director of Business Analysis at Glaxo Wellcome from 1995-1998. Before that, Mr. Mossinghoff filled various positions of increasing responsibility in business development, new product planning, strategic planning, finance and operations at Roche Holding Ltd., Basel, Switzerland and Nutley, NJ. Mr. Mossinghoff received a BA degree in Economics from the University of Virginia and an MBA in Financial Management & Analysis from George Mason University. He is a member of the Licensing Executives Society, National Association of Corporate Directors and is the company's Biotechnology Industry Association representative.

The Emerging Position of Specialty Pharmaceutical Firms

Dr. Anthony H. Wild
Chairman & CEO
MedPointe Pharmaceuticals, Inc.

Carving Out a Niche in the Marketplace

The pharmaceutical industry is quite a special one. It is probably the most research-intensive industry in today's society. Since research is so expensive, the industry needs to be global to recoup its investment. Also, it makes products which people would rather not use; being healthy is preferable to being ill. Finally, the industry interacts in a uniquely indirect fashion: its main "customers" are physicians who neither use their products nor pay for them. The ultimate "user" is the patient who, in general, doesn't decide what to consume and often does not pay for it. All in all, it is an odd state of affairs.

The industry's economics are also odd: unlike most other fields, there is no dominant position of a just a few companies. There is no GE, Microsoft or Procter & Gamble. Why is this? Simply because there are literally many hundreds of different diseases and illnesses. To treat them, there are several thousands of pharmaceutical products. As a result, there are many pharmaceutical companies which develop, manufacture and sell drugs. Even Pfizer, the largest pharma company in the world and a veritable giant within the industry, has only a 10 percent share, much of which has been garnered by gobbling up other firms such as Warner-Lambert and Pharmacia though acquisitions. Many companies choose to specialize and are active in only a few areas of medicine. Some companies are famous for cancer drugs, for example; others focus on the skin or gastro-intestinal disorders. What most companies strive to achieve is to become an expert in one or more fields where they develop real expertise and forge strong relationships with physicians and other medical professionals.

Although there are no dominant players in our industry, it is consolidating as costs of R&D escalate and companies seek economies of scale. Even bigger companies can only afford to concentrate on bigger

THE EMERGING POSITION OF SPECIALTY PHARMACEUTICAL FIRMS

opportunities. This leaves gaps: less common diseases, smaller products, special patient types and so on. Therein lies the opportunity for smaller niche players such as MedPointe.

We are a new company, founded in October 2001. We specialize in the U.S. prescription-pharmaceutical market; we do not sell diagnostic devices or other medical products. All our products are branded, with sales resulting from prescriptions written by physicians. We do not market generic copies. The distinction is an important one: once a patent expires and a drug is copied, the relationship between the physician and the drug's manufacturer is lost. Generic companies do not visit physicians, they simply manufacture and supply to pharmacies. The pharmacist decides from which source to purchase a particular generic drug. Any doctor who writes a prescription for, say, penicillin, has no idea which manufacturer will actually supply the product to his/her patient. In MedPointe's case, all of our sales result from an active dialogue between our company's representatives and the physician.

As a small company, we are labeled as one of the so-called "specialty pharmaceutical firms," a term coined by Wall Street a decade ago to describe emerging niche players which exploit smaller opportunities, usually without doing any basic research. We do not discover new drugs, rather we license in or acquire drugs from other companies. In addition, we have a development laboratory where we work on new formulations and presentations—changing flavors, improving tablets, coming out with different forms, and getting combinations of active ingredients. We focus on the smaller products that don't sell hundreds of millions of dollars but rather tend to get neglected by the bigger companies.

Our Specialty Pharmaceuticals

At MedPointe, we specialize in two main areas in particular. One focus is the treatment of allergies and respiratory disorders such as cough, cold, and so on. We have a number of products, but our biggest and fastest growing product is ASTELIN, which is an antihistamine in nasal-spray form. It is a treatment for rhinitis, or congestion of the nasal passages, caused by allergens such as pollen and animal fur or environmental irritants such as smoke fumes. It is the only prescription nasal-spray antihistamine on the US market. All other antihistamines are tablets taken orally. What is neat about ASTELIN is that it's sprayed up the nose thus providing immediate cooling relief. It is also the only antihistamine approved by the FDA for non-allergic rhinitis. We tend to think of rhinitis as caused by pollens and molds in the air, but only about one third of rhinitis is actually allergic, while about two thirds of rhinitis is either partially or totally non-allergic in origin. It could be caused by smoke, exhaust fumes from cars, perfumes, paint or even cold weather. Many people suffer from this condition, which is called vasomotor rhinitis, something which is not particularly easy to treat. A typical oral antihistamine such as Claritin simply doesn't work in this indication – ASTELIN does.

Our second area of focus is on drugs for neurology and the central nervous system. FELBATOL is an example of that. It is regarded by the FDA and the medical profession as a medically-essential drug for certain types of refractory epilepsy, which do not respond to other treatment. Because it is a powerful drug, it needs to be used very carefully: it is prescribed by epilepsy specialists only and its use monitored carefully. As such, it is a good example of a small product that will never become a large moneymaker and would be of no interest to a large company.

ASTELIN and FELBATOL are two examples which help to define what I mean by specialty pharmaceuticals.

Risks in the Pharmaceutical Industry

Risk is an important consideration in our industry. After all, we make products which enter and interfere with the workings of the human body. The perfect drug is one which treats a certain illness or condition well, in a highly selective manner. That way, you have a minimum of side effects. If you want a drug to reduce blood pressure, for example, it should reduce blood pressure quickly, smoothly, just the right amount (which means neither too much nor too little), without anything else untoward happening. We hope for no side effects such as a headache, an upset stomach, or worse.

Unfortunately, because the human body is so complex, it is very difficult to design a molecule that interacts so exquisitely well with the very part of the body that you want without affecting anything else. Some drugs are very good at doing that and can work safely, sometimes in a dramatic way. Other drugs may be medically important but are more toxic. For example, some high-blood pressure medicines cause lethargy or cold hands, some cough-cold drugs cause drowsiness or a dry mouth.

Thus there are scientific and medical risks associated with any product, which we minimize by getting to know it extremely well during its development by testing it very thoroughly. We need to understand everything so that we can accurately and completely describe in the labeling the way the product works and how it should be used. This labeling is worked out in great detail together with the FDA and needs to be approved by them. This in turn demands a close and collaborative relationship with the FDA.

As I said, there will always be risks with any pharmaceutical. By their very nature, new products are less well known and carry higher risks than well-understood, well-characterized products that have been used for years. Specialty pharma companies as a group tend to run lower levels of risk because they are rarely involved with new products. Acquiring mature products which have been well tried for a number of years is a medically less-risky proposition.

However, just like any other business, specialty companies like MedPointe do bear business risks. Indeed being smaller and more dependent on individual products, we bear potentially larger risks than large companies with broad product portfolios. Also, as an industry, we invest large amounts of capital to acquire products and typically have significantly more debt in our balance sheets than big pharma companies. We therefore worry about whether we are going to get a return on our investments? That is why we have to do our homework carefully before making an acquisition. Can we grow this product? If not, then we should not invest in the opportunity. A series of poor decisions could rapidly lead to bankruptcy but then, that's not unique to pharmaceuticals. In evaluating opportunities, it is important to work not only inside the company but also to go outside and talk to healthcare professionals. The better job that we do there — the more thorough, the more professional, the more careful job we do— the lower the risks of a project.

Working Effectively

Our marketplace has become highly competitive in recent years; there are many other new specialty pharmaceutical companies. In order to be successful, we need quite simply to do a better job than the others.

How do we do this? Let me highlight four areas:

First, we have built a financially strong company: a strong balance sheet, strong financial backing with good access to additional capital, robust financial systems that keep information at our fingertips.

Second, we try to stay focused. We evaluate many opportunities which we decline. We want to stay in areas that we know well and where we can compete effectively and win. We do not want to clash head on with a large company and get out-gunned.

Third, we focus maniacally on execution: getting the job done. Whether this is the hunting team scouring for opportunities, the deal team which puts together the transaction, the marketing team which builds the strategy, the sales team which communicates effectively to our target audience, the supply-chain team which builds or acquires the products or any of the support functions within the company, everything boils down to excellence in execution.

All of the above lead to my fourth differentiator: people. Nothing gets done without people and we spend an awful lot of time on this. I see my own job as leader of the company as one of recruiting, retaining, developing and motivating my team. If I succeed in doing this, as well as making sure they understand our mission and have the tools to accomplish it, the job will get done and done well.

The Importance of the Physicians

The principal way that we go about marketing our products is through face-to-face dialogue with physicians. Clearly the physician is very important. We have a team of well-trained people who go out and visit with them. That's their job — to inform them of the product, to provide information and documentation on the product, and to encourage a physician to test out a product. A representative will then typically visit that physician some weeks later to continue the dialogue. In which types of patients does the product work best? How should the product be used or not used? From this dialogue we get a lot of feedback in the head office to enable us to modify programs or come up with new ideas and further developments.

As I mentioned before, dealing with prescription products means that every sale comes from a prescription written by physician. Unlike the consumer business, you're not dealing with hundreds of thousands or millions of customers. You're dealing with a few thousand very highly trained and demanding "customers." Each physician is very important, which is why we tend to visit physicians quite regularly and make sure that we provide them with as much information as they need. Should they call and want more information, we make sure that we are very service-oriented and get information there very quickly. We sometimes supplement our own information flow with meetings where primary care (family) practitioners can hear more about a particular treatment, not just from us, but from local specialists who know the product. We might invite half a dozen or a dozen GPs in Pittsburgh, for example, to listen to a professor from the University of Pittsburgh talking about the treatment of rhinitis and how ASTELIN may work in that treatment. They hear not just from the company, but also from doctors who use the product and understand it well.

A Successful Pharmaceutical Product

In general terms, pharmaceutical treatment of a medical condition is the most elegant and most preferred medical treatment in almost every case.

The Emerging Position of Specialty Pharmaceutical Firms

If you can avoid hospital visits, or operations, for example, that is wonderful. There are many drugs available today which have revolutionized medical treatment— if you think about the effectiveness of products such as Prozac and similar antidepressants, for instance, the number of people who have to be admitted to mental facilities is dramatically lower than it was ten or fifteen years ago. Many patients, for the first time in their lives, can lead a normal existence because of modern drugs. I know we tend to see and hear a lot of criticism about the pharmaceutical industry. It is said that we are a capitalistic industry making profit off of sick people, but in reality, we should be proud of what we've been able to achieve in the last fifty years, which is effectively the time span of the modern pharmaceutical industry. We are helping to save lives and improve the quality of life.

As I mentioned before, the ideal drug is one that works well, with a minimum of side effects. Also, it is nice to take something once which cures the problem; antibiotics are good examples here – kill the bug and the patient recovers. We are always looking for such "silver bullets" but, unfortunately, the majority of illnesses stem from genetic problems leading to some internal imbalance and require chronic treatment. Pills can control high blood pressure or gout well, for example, but need to be taken for life. Stop the treatment and the disorder bounces back.

Drugs should also be easy to use. A small tablet that has to be swallowed once a day is much better than ten large tablets that have to be taken six times a day. It's up to the ingenuity of the scientists to find molecules that are more active in the body so that they can be used in smaller doses. Also, a drug which can be absorbed from the gastrointestinal tract is preferable so it can be given orally in tablet or liquid form. However, many drugs are either destroyed when they are swallowed — they break down in the stomach — or they are not absorbed and have to be given by some other route.

Some drugs are injected, some drugs are inhaled, and some drugs are squirted up the nose. There are different ways of administering drugs, but the easiest is generally the oral route. Whichever route is used, the less frequently it is given, the better. If you have to have an injection once a week or once a month, that's preferable to having an injection every day. It is also preferable to have an injection that can be injected into the fatty tissue or subcutaneous tissue of the body. That's much easier to do than injecting into the muscle. Injection into subcutaneous tissue is something patients themselves can do. A good example here is diabetes and insulin injections. Injecting into the muscle is something only medically trained people can do. A drug that has to be injected into a vein is even trickier. In trying to develop products we, and every pharmaceutical company, look for a drug that works well, is safe to use, and is easy to administer.

The other factor, of course, is that drugs should be affordable. High research costs always mean there is a hurdle to jump over. In addition, many drugs are extraordinarily difficult and expensive to manufacture. Some of them may cost thousands of dollars a year as a result.

Public Perception vs. Doctor Adoption of Drugs

Public perception about medicines depends very much on the type of drug and where it is in its life cycle.

Usually a new drug is first heard about by leading researchers during the development process. Once a company is satisfied with all of its laboratory testing, it then needs to carry out a whole program of clinical research to test how well a product works in man. In this way, it generates the data required as part of the new drug application process, which goes to the FDA for approval. Such data packages will contain details of the treatment of hundreds and usually thousands of patients.

Many physicians will have used the product as part of that clinical research. Typically, they are experts in their fields, with a lot of experience in both treating patients as well as in research and who publish papers in leading medical journals.

Following a drug's approval by the FDA, early usage is often by the very physicians who tested it during research since they already know it and are comfortable about using it. Usage then spreads to their own colleagues who either hear about it through them or read about the product in medical journals. You often find the most rapid adoption of a product is from other specialists. Then the word spreads to internists and family practitioners. It is a cascading process that moves down from the national opinion leaders, to the leading specialists, to regional specialists, to internists and family practitioners. This process is of course facilitated by the sales force of the company selling the product. Information, instructions, support materials and samples help physicians feel comfortable about using a product. Most practicing physicians have little time to sit and read all of the medical journals and thus rely heavily on well-trained and informed company representatives to bring them information on new products.

The adoption process varies with the type of product. A totally new type of drug is typically going to be used with more caution than a new variant of an existing class, such as a penicillin or an antihistamine. Drugs with challenging side effects or those which are difficult to administer are going to be used with a lot more caution. Products which everyone regards as pretty safe are likely to be adopted quite quickly by primary care doctors with much more hesitation being shown where major side effects are possible.

Traditionally, patients have not played an important role in this process; indeed, they typically have had a pretty low level of awareness of what they were being treated with. Some patients may have heard about a particular drug from a friend or relative but, unless they took the trouble to read medical journals, they had little or no access to information on their drugs – certainly little was volunteered by the average physician. This has changed dramatically over the last decade and there are three reasons for this. Firstly, many more patients are better educated and willing to ask questions, even challenge their physicians. The lay media focus much more on healthcare than they used to; we are exposed every day to issues surrounding medical treatments on TV and in newspapers and magazines. Secondly, the advent of the Internet has made access to a wealth of information very easy. As a result, many patients are doing a lot of their own research and thinking through treatment options themselves. Thirdly, and perhaps most interestingly, we have witnessed the new phenomenon of direct-to-consumer advertising since the FDA relaxed restrictions over the past ten years or so. The incentive for this came originally from pharmaceutical companies who saw this as a way of supplementing their traditional promotional messages to physicians. DTC advertising makes patients aware of effective new drugs and encourages them to go to their doctors and ask about the drugs. The industry's goal was clear: to accelerate the adoption of new products and it has become a big business. Since 2000, over $2 billion has been spent annually on DTC advertising.

In the early days of DTC, many physicians complained. So used to being the sole decision maker without criticism or challenge, many did not communicate well with their patients about details of their treatments, let alone about treatment options. A typical information flow might be "your blood pressure is too high; I want you to start taking these little pink pills." As a result, they didn't respond well to questions coming from patients in the early days of DTC, for example "Doctor, how are you treating my high blood pressure – am I on an ACE inhibitor or a beta blocker? Which is safer? Wouldn't I be better off on XYZ?" One of the first heavily advertised products was the antihistamine Claritin. Many hay fever patients would go in and say that they had been reading about this wonderful new drug Claritin, and that they wanted to use it "instead of that old sedating Benadryl." Many doctors reacted negatively to that type of pressure, at least initially.

That has gradually changed, however. I've seen a number of recent studies indicating that a majority of physicians are in favor of DTC, and the FDA recently came out with a signal of positive support. A better educated, better informed patient is a better patient overall. Physicians are now much more open to suggestions or at least to an active dialogue with their patients.

The one area of controversy remains the cost of pharmaceuticals. Most DTC advertising is devoted to new products which tend to be more expensive than older ones or generic alternatives. Managed-care organizations sometimes resent the pressure to pay for products that they feel are too expensive. Thus the biggest argument against DTC advertising today is that it helps to drive up healthcare costs.

Challenges in the Industry

This leads me to one of the biggest challenges we are facing as a society – the cost of healthcare. This has steadily risen over the last thirty years and has now reached around 14 percent of GDP. Employers, individuals and the government are struggling with this increasing burden. Reasons for this increase include the increasing population, the demographic shift towards more elderly folks, medical advances themselves (i.e. treatments which did not exist earlier, or else newer and more expensive options), better educated patients with higher demands for quantity and quality of treatment and, sadly, also the increasingly litigious nature of our society whereby the legal profession encourages us to sue at every opportunity.

Exacerbating this pain is the fact that the mechanisms for reimbursing people for their healthcare costs are inadequate – 40 million people have no health insurance at all. Quite frankly, as a European, I find it extraordinary that the leading nation of the modern world tolerates such a state of affairs. The fact that senior citizens on Medicare have been denied access to drugs only adds fuel to the flames of debate.

Solutions are complex and difficult to find; no one seems to have the political courage to propose bold reforms. Apportioning blame, on the other hand, is easier and makes one feel better. Since the doctor and the nurse still occupy much respected roles in our society, finger-pointing turns instead to other areas such as managed care and, above all, pharmaceuticals: "how can they charge $1 for a little white pill that costs only 5¢ to make"; "to make profits off of sick people." The fact that the pharmaceutical industry is the only global and obviously capitalistic part of healthcare makes us an easy target – never mind that the drug bill makes up only 10¢ of every healthcare dollar.

As a result, doctors, pharmacists, managed care institutions, even patients focus on the cost of drugs in isolation and debate how they can be reduced, or at least contained. Yet, at the same time, most people will recognize that medicines are potentially the most cost-effective therapeutic alternative around; a week of antibiotics costs much less than a week in the hospital. Even a lifelong regimen of a cholesterol-reducing drug is much cheaper than the costs of intensive care treatment following a heart attack, or the cost of bypass surgery.

Looking into the future, new discoveries in pharmaceutical research may well drive drug costs up instead of down. This is because there are many illnesses and diseases today for which there is no effective drug. Take the treatment of a migraine, for example – drugs available today are relatively ineffective. They may work in some patients, but overall society needs better treatment options for migraines. There are estimated to be over thirty million migraine sufferers in this country today. The current market for drugs sold today to treat migraines is a little under $2 billion a year. However, according to estimates that have been well researched, the total current cost to society for migraines is $12 to $14 billion. This includes not just direct medical costs, but also the costs associated with disability – days off from work by patients or family members who stay home to take care of relatives, and the like. So, wouldn't it be wonderful to come up with a "silver bullet" which easily treated all migraine patients? This could save society not just a lot of suffering, but also a lot of money, right?

Let's say we come up with a wonder drug to treat migraines, and it becomes incredibly successful. This might then become a $3 or $4 billion dollar drug. All of a sudden, the cost of healthcare for the treatment of migraines spirals up from $2 billion to $5 or $6 billion. Everyone would be up in arms and Congress would call it a disgrace and call for the fat cats of pharma to do something to reduce prices. Managed care would say they are not going to reimburse it. Everyone, of course, is forgetting that the country is saving possibly $10 billion because migraine sufferers are now fit and healthy and are not taking time off from work. That equation is not being written. Politicians and healthcare experts are not willing, or are not able, to make the connection between those two worlds. Very often a new drug enables a new type of treatment which did not exist before and, in the short term, that represents a new cost, which as I said, people complain about rather than praise this wonderful advance.

This debate is going on and on in Washington, and it is getting louder and louder. They are looking at healthcare costs alone and what can be done to contain and reduce them. As I said, because the pharmaceutical industry is global and profitable, we have become the popular whipping boy, which is grossly unfair. Mind you, we have not helped ourselves much by our poor handling of the public relations dimension over the years. If we are going to overcome this negative perception, we must be able to demonstrate to the world at large that we are a cost-effective part of the solution rather than being the problem.

Challenges of Healthcare in General

Today, healthcare in this country costs between $5,000 and $6,000 a year per person on average. Total GDP per capita is around $36,000. Hence, at least on the surface, this should be affordable. Ultimately, each individual must pay this, directly by paying bills or indirectly by paying taxes. The question is how to spread the burden in the most equitable manner. This is the role of health insurance and, unfortunately, this is something which today is quite simply not working.

There must be a better way of providing a decent level of health insurance to everybody. I personally feel that we have to get away from company sponsored employee insurance. Some companies cannot afford to offer health insurance and there are a lot of people who are self-employed, move from one company to another, or have lost their job. I think society needs a type of personal health insurance that an individual or family keeps, indeed manages. It would remain portable and stay with the individual as he or she moves. Such insurance should of course cover pharmaceuticals as well. I envisage a system where employers would have to contribute, contributions would be tax-deductible and the government would step in with subsidies during times of unemployment. Regulations would ensure coverage but we might well see premiums varying with lifestyle; not only would smokers pay more, but also possibly those who are overweight or who will not comply with treatment. Such a universal system could remove a lot of the emotions from the healthcare debate.

What appears to be lacking today is an honest and open debate about healthcare and its costs. We have now reached an age in our society where a lot more is possible than is affordable. If you twist an ankle or damage an elbow, and you go into a physician, you probably would have a CAT scan or an MRI, which costs several hundred dollars. Is this good medicine? Should every patient have a total body scan, for example, every time they come in to see their doctor? Clearly not — that would be overkill. But, if you did have a total body scan every time you went to your doctor, you would definitely find out things that might save your life. Economists tell us this is not cost effective. At what age do you stop giving people heart or kidney transplants?

Many of those types of questions are no longer medical but social or socio-economic. Managed care is struggling with many issues; every time they try to ration healthcare, patients get upset because they want the best possible healthcare. There is a feeling of entitlement about healthcare. As a result, many plans have moved towards a cost-sharing structure with patients sharing meaningfully in the cost of any treatment. The three-tier co-pay system for drugs is a good example here: First tier drugs, typically generics, cost a patient only five or ten dollars. Preferred-formulary branded drugs in second tier cost maybe fifteen to twenty dollars, but off-formulary drugs in the third tier may set back a patient thirty-five to fifty dollars in co-payment. This structure encourages a dialogue between the physician, pharmacist and patient, with the patient making the final choice between the latest in drug therapy – at a cost – or electing to take the cheaper generic. In the old days every patient wanted the best and most expensive because there was no economic consequence of such a decision.

Industry-wide Changes

Coming back to our industry, a couple of important things have changed in recent years. One is that research is becoming more and more difficult. Even though companies are spending a lot more now on basic research than they used to (now up to 20 percent of sales), productivity is down as they operate ever closer to the frontiers of science. The so-called low hanging fruits have already been plucked. Companies are not able to introduce enough new products to maintain decent growth rates, especially during a time when much of the earlier successes are now going off patent and generic copies are eroding the original business.

Generics can be very cheap because no research or marketing costs are involved and the cost of manufacturing is not high. In recent years, pressure from managed care has ensured a very rapid switch to generic prescribing. Eighty or ninety percent of the volume can be lost to generics within weeks of patent expiration. In summary, many of the big companies are struggling; they are losing business from their older products and are not able to introduce new products quickly enough.

As a result, overall growth rates in the US pharmaceutical industry have been coming down; in the last year or so, it has dropped down into the single digits with annual price increases no more than 2 or 3 percent.

Overall, therefore, economic pressures are much greater in our industry than they used to be; growth rates and margins have come down. There have been quite a few significant mergers and acquisitions in the quest for economies of scale and increased growth rates.

These challenges make me excited because therein lies the opportunity for small companies such as MedPointe. We relish the challenge. Just look at ASTELIN as an example – the antihistamine market is declining quite significantly and there are pressures from Managed care to use OTC rather than prescription products. Yet, with its very specific and different positioning, ASTELIN is, by far, the fastest-growing antihistamine product on the market. We saw the changes coming and moved hard and fast – we thrive on change.

We will continue to see the pharmaceutical market consolidate. With this, we will also see a parallel expansion of the specialty segment. Long live the difference!

Anthony H. Wild, Ph.D., is Chairman and CEO of MedPointe Inc., a privately held specialty pharmaceutical company that develops, markets and sells branded prescription products. He brings a wealth of experience gained in a global career of 30 years in the pharmaceutical industry.

Prior to joining MedPointe, Tony served as Executive Vice President of Warner-Lambert and President of its Pharmaceutical Sector (until the merger with Pfizer in June 2000), with worldwide responsibility for Warner-Lambert's pharmaceutical commercial operations and research and development. Under his leadership, Warner-Lambert's pharmaceutical business grew from $2.1 billion in sales with 14,000 employees in 1995 to an estimated $9.5 billion in 2000 with 21,000 employees and a $1.3 billion R&D budget. During this period, Tony oversaw a number of acquisitions including those of Jouveinal (France), Hickson (Eire) and Agouron (La Jolla), the setting up of the US joint-venture with Sankyo and that of the Pfizer global LIPITOR partnership.

Prior to joining Warner-Lambert in 1995 (initially as President of Parke-Davis North America before assuming global responsibilities in 1996), Tony spent 22 years with Schering-Plough Corporation in Switzerland, Sweden, South Africa, the Netherlands, United States and culminating as President of Schering-Plough's Japanese operations, a $500 million business, including a complex web of licensee/ licensor partnerships with major Japanese companies. Prior to that, he was employed at Sandoz AG in Basel, Switzerland, as a Development Chemist, where he worked on optimization and simulation of chemical processes.

Dr. Wild is a member of the Board of Advisors to the Joseph L. Mailman School of Public Health at Columbia University, a Trustee of the Healthcare Institute of New Jersey, past Chairman of the International Section of Pharmaceutical Research and Manufacturers of America, and past Governor of the American Chamber of Commerce in Japan.

Dr. Wild graduated from the University of York with a B.A. honors degree in Chemistry and received a Ph.D. in Physical Chemistry from the University of Cambridge (Churchill College), both in the U.K.

Do One Thing Really Well:
Finding a Niche in Specialty Pharma

Dr. Cameron Durrant
President
PediaMed – The Pediatrics Company™

Introduction

The adage – *Do one thing and do it well* – essentially has been lost on the pharmaceutical industry, as giant corporations are swallowing smaller pharma outfits in the pursuit of additional sources of revenue. In the process these companies are trying to do many things well with varying degrees of success. Over the past decade, the pharmaceutical industry has been coalescing into mega players, primarily through mergers and acquisitions.

The image of Big Pharma may be no better than that of Big Tobacco or, now, Big Food. But what of the dedication to improving healthcare? Of bringing to market the best products to eradicate disease and increase life span? These noble goals exist within even the largest pharmaceutical companies, which is why lifesaving medications are often greatly discounted for poorer countries and improvements are made to drugs within the same class to better serve all patients.

No matter the size, most pharmaceutical companies have at least one physician on staff. The Hippocratic Oath is well ingrained in those physicians, and they carry the intention to heal even into corporate America. One of the best ways to heal, to improve healthcare and improve quality of life for patients, is to *Do one thing and do it really well*. Small specialty pharmaceutical companies are carving independent niches for themselves and adhering to specific missions in pursuit of that maxim.

Big Pharma has brought to market some of the most advanced medicines available today and spends more on research than the United States federal government. In order to sustain large-scale growth and hefty staff rosters, blockbuster drugs remain the pursuit of the largest manufacturers. There are customer and therapeutic areas that are overlooked because it does not make financial sense for Big Pharma to invest the hundreds of millions of dollars it takes to bring a drug to market. But these disease areas can often be very profitable for smaller, specialty pharmaceutical companies and can satisfy unmet medical needs. It is the smaller companies, those who have the resources and drive to compete, that are fast becoming the backbone of egalitarian medicine in this country and abroad.

Seizing Opportunities: Specialty Pharmaceuticals vs. Big Companies

Just as the practice of medicine has been subdivided by the proliferation of specialization, specialty pharmaceutical companies that concentrate on a particular therapeutic category, such as dermatology or cardiology, or on a particular physician subgroup, are flourishing. PediaMed – The Pediatrics Company, for example, focuses on pediatricians and their patient population. While other companies market individual products to pediatricians, few are solely focused on this audience.

Big pharmaceutical companies are facing patent expiration of some blockbuster products and many also have relatively dry pipelines. According to recent data from Windhover's Strategic Intelligence Systems databases, Big Pharma held 40 percent to 45 percent of all Phase II and Phase III molecules during the period of 2001 to 2002, but that figure dropped to only 26 percent in 2003 due in part to late phase failures and sell-offs. A financially viable big pharmaceutical company is only as strong as its drug pipeline. Without a constant stream of new products, the future looks somewhat grim for many of the big players. There are many pathways to developing a pipeline, including product acquisitions from other companies, clinical research and development, and collaboration with academic institutions. But there are limits to the relative attractiveness and ease of such pathways.

In addition to the pressure of patents expiring, there is the pressure from government and patient lobbies, and the sheer challenge of managing on such a large scale. Pfizer has somewhere around 150,000 employees. Managing that many people is difficult; it puts additional pressure on earnings growth. One way to relieve that earnings growth pressure is through the acquisition of another company, but there are only so many companies you can acquire before the model runs out of steam. Also, with acquisitions come other challenges such as employee redundancies, increased overhead and sometimes competing products. Collectively, these challenges have traditional big pharmaceuticals heading for a crisis. Building sustainable competitive advantage and delivering consistent earnings growth by M&A only is clearly untenable.

Big Pharma must look at ways to become leaner, which may mean retaining core intellectual capital and outsourcing just about everything else. Collaborations with smaller organizations – biotech, genomics, and proteomics companies – will become more and more common. That is where specialty pharmaceuticals play an active role. As the big companies increasingly concentrate on fewer, but bigger products, there will be smaller drugs that fail to register on their radar screens. Smaller specialty pharmas are in a position to further develop and market, through line extensions and reformulation options, the leave-behind compounds that Big Pharma chooses to drop either in development or which may be already approved, but under promoted. Specialty pharmaceutical companies also have less redundancy within the employee base and a focus on a highly specific target audience, meaning sales representatives can systematically educate and develop relationships with those healthcare professionals.

Establishing a Niche

PediaMed – The Pediatrics Company, for example, develops and markets prescription pharmaceuticals with a focus on improving the health and well-being of children. The company is focused on being the best pediatrics pharmaceutical company in the world. Having this specialization and clear vision helps the company to build stronger customer relationships by better understanding the needs of pediatricians than those with transient interest in this physician population. Simply put, our team has the time to build and maintain valuable contacts within the pediatric field.

Additionally, this is a relatively small customer group on which to focus attention. Approximately 37,000 office-based pediatricians practice in the United States. With all resources mobilized toward that number of customers, fewer representatives and a tighter infrastructure are necessary than if the target audience were primary care, which number upwards of 420,000 customers. By contrast, there are 7,000 medical oncologists in the United States, and many companies focus on them to the point where the excessive information becomes like white noise, barely registering during a few moments of time in the oncologist's office. The resource investment in the field does not mean a guaranteed return. The efficiency and expertise of a specialized sales force saves much needed capital that can be earmarked for product acquisitions or development.

Because not many companies focus their work on pediatric medicines, the competitive environment is significantly less intense than for other medical specialties, but it is also a much larger market than people think, generating about $20 billion in the United States alone (source Kalorama). And this number is set to grow. Medco recently published a study that showed the under-18 age group to be the fastest-growing population segment in the country. Coupled with the aging Baby Boomers, at the two ends of the age spectrum the nation's population is creating an inverted bell curve of medical need.

Regulatory and Legislative Landscape Changes

Compounding this need, nearly 80 percent of medicines prescribed to children are not approved for pediatric use by the Food and Drug Administration. Primarily, these medicines are studied and approved for use in adult populations, eventually making their way to children simply because there are no alternatives. The FDA Modernization Act of 1997 provided drug companies with, among other incentives, six months additional marketing exclusivity for pediatric indications. But most large companies lacked the motivation to pursue such indications and divert resources to small markets.

The Pediatric Research Equity Act of 2003 is a crucial piece of legislation. It mandates that pharmaceutical companies must evaluate medicines that could be used by children with the same critical and objective standards as for medicines studied for the adult population. The law requires that pharmaceutical companies who do not wish to test drugs in children bear the burden of proving that the drug will not be used by children. Signed into law in December, 2003, the Pediatric Research Equity Act effects all NDAs submitted to the FDA since April 1, 1999.

The Pediatric Rule, also established in 2003, supplements the Best Pharmaceuticals for Children Act, a law that provides financial incentives to pharmaceutical companies voluntarily testing drugs in children. The Pediatric Rule requires companies that are not testing for the exclusivity rights to ensure their drugs are safe for pediatric populations.

The Paradox for Big Pharma – Avoiding a PR Crisis

The American Academy of Pediatrics estimates that, until the passage of the Pediatric Research Equity Act and the Pediatric Rule, only a small fraction of all drugs marketed in the US were tested in pediatric patients, regardless of whether they were prescribed to children or not. And the younger the child, the less information had been documented about adverse events.

This is important not only in that it highlights the safety needs of pediatric patients, but that companies that develop medicines for children are given the opportunity to spotlight their serious R&D capabilities. As physicians and parents become aware of the differences between child-size doses of adult medications and drugs truly developed for children, specialty pharmaceutical companies like PediaMed will gain stature – and market share – within the industry. The result will mean millions of dollars in revenue.

The recent legislation allows pharmaceutical companies to add six months of life to its patent if it submits pediatric data for safety and efficacy, which present clear opportunity to the industry. Market exclusivity in this age of generic competition and foreign reimportation of medicines can be a boon for smaller companies to generate revenue. An additional six months added to a patent for a product that has reached the end of its lifecycle could translate to hundreds of millions of dollars in additional sales. However, for large pharmaceutical companies who have products with pediatric indications, diverting resources to commercialize that indication may not be cost-effective when compared to the billions of dollars in potential sales from existing and pipeline adult medications. Big Pharma may go through the necessary testing to gain six months of patent extension, but not have the desire or ability to properly market the product to the pediatric community. Or products may not have the opportunity to gain additional patent life because of the company's inexperience in conducting pediatric clinical trials. These are the situations where a partnership with a specialty pediatric pharmaceutical company would benefit the originator of the drug. The sales team that already has relationships with the target pediatrician audience could, for relatively little additional cost, detail other companies' pediatric indications, with both companies sharing profit. The educational benefit for the underserved physician market is also a consideration, resulting in improved patient care.

Even without specific legislation to boost the need for specialty pharma, there exists vast opportunity for growth in other subpopulations. The geriatric market, for example, is growing at a clip. According to the American Geriatrics Society, by 2030, it is projected that one in five people will be age 65 or older, essentially doubling the older population to 70 million. Coupled with advances in medications for Alzheimer's, Parkinson's, and a host of other typically late in life diseases, specialty pharmaceutical companies can position themselves as viable partners with connections in the geriatric target audiences. Certified geriatricians make up a very small percentage of the physicians in the United States, but family practitioners and internists see much of the aging population and so require the knowledge to treat them with the most up-to-date information. This can include special dosing for older or frailer adults, increased awareness of drug interactions and formulations that are easier on a taxed digestive system. Again, this shared knowledge and niche expertise can improve healthcare for older adults and the bottom line for specialty pharmaceutical companies.

The Method to Success

A company must keep in communication with the people, its physicians, and other healthcare professionals, like pharmacists, nurse practitioners, and physician assistants. Managed care companies, HMOs and state Medicaid plans are also stakeholders in the pharmaceutical industry and need to be communicated with regularly. Pharmaceutical companies need to reach out to all of those customers with educational and marketing efforts. But education is a two-way street. While we bring our focused pediatric expertise to the physician and the parent, we also learn from these caretakers what is in the best interest of a child patient.

Part of our development process is taking existing medicines and reformulating them based on our research and shared information with physicians and parents. We make medications better tasting, change the dosage, and sometimes put them into different formulations that may have greater appeal for children. For example, some medicines can be put into chewable tablets. Children often prefer chewable tablets to pills that must be swallowed. Something as simple as a new flavor can improve compliance on the part of the child, reduce frustration for parents, and aid pediatricians in treating their patients. The best medication in the world will not work if the child refuses to take it.

All of this research and thought adds up to profits. By providing thoughtful, improved options, a specialty pharmaceutical company can rise above the din of its competitors consistently enough to become the prescriber's first choice. That trust between pharma and physician is too important to public health and mutual success to be understated. With an eye toward future acquisitions, reformulations and original development, the potential for growth is nearly limitless.

Changes and Trends in the Industry

For the first time in history, patients and consumers are taking an active, if not equal, role in their own healthcare. Physicians and patients are learning from each other and fostering partnerships to maintain the patient's health. Some of this increase in patient education can be attributed to the dawn of the Internet, but also to the significant contributions of pharmaceutical companies funding educational programs and materials. The result is a better informed patient who no longer is subject to the paternalistic trappings of the old guard.

To improve outcomes of the practicing physician, better and more inventive scientific methods have been developed that enable the pharmaceutical companies to investigate more compounds in less time. Pharma benefits from reduced time to market with valuable medicines, and physicians benefit from the availability of even more effective drug options. New technologies will continue to accelerate companies' ability to discover new drugs.

One outcome of all this technology is the rising cost of healthcare. Pricing of pharmaceuticals have come under intense scrutiny, and will continue to be the scapegoat for much of the healthcare industry's ills. Americans tend to blame high healthcare costs on drugs and perceive greed for profits as the sole motivator for pharmaceutical companies. If companies can meet customer needs effectively, logic follows that profits will be generated, which is then channeled into producing new, more effective products. While profits are important because they are part of a virtuous cycle of channeling funds into additional R&D, they are not the only factor.

Study after study has demonstrated that the increase in pharmaceutical spending is primarily due to increased use. IMS Health found that, although spending on drugs increased by 14.7 percent in 2000, only 3.9 percent was attributable to an increase in price. In addition, increased use of pharmaceuticals may make overall health spending decrease because drugs may shorten or prevent costly hospital stays.

The escalating cost of medicine is also something we see in the United States, which, not coincidentally, is where the lion's share of development and innovation are undertaken. Without the research borne in the US, modern medication around the world would not be the lifesaving gift it is. In other parts of the world, where healthcare systems have implemented pricing and profit controls, drug discovery and healthcare innovation have been stifled.

The Cycle of Increased Costs

Of course, there are more immediate issues that are driving up healthcare costs. As society becomes ever more litigious, doctors are forced to practice defensive medicine, which is often not in the patient's best interest, and pharmaceutical companies must debate whether the benefit of bringing a drug to market outweighs the potential litigation risk. Tort reform is sorely needed to protect the health of the nation.

According to Walter Olson, senior fellow at the Manhattan Institute and noted author, the current "jackpot" justice approach to medical malpractice means that the average doctor will be sued twice during his or her career. In 2002, 13 of the top 100 verdicts were medical liability cases, and the rewards were astronomical. Three such verdicts awarded amounts of $94 million, $90 million, and $62 million.

Now trial lawyers have begun to target the pharmaceutical industry. The plaintiff's bar has always loved the theory of market share liability, but in the pharmaceutical arena, courts have limited it to generics. Trial attorneys in America's medicine chest, New Jersey, are trying to expand the theory to branded pharmaceuticals as well.

Under the theory of market share liability, a person injured by a product, but who cannot identify the manufacturer, gets to sue and collect from each manufacturer in proportion to its market share. Once injury is established, the theory shifts the burden of proof to the defendant. The plaintiff does not have to prove beyond a preponderance of the evidence that brand X injured him; the manufacturer of brand X has to prove that brand X could not have injured the plaintiff. Expanding this theory to the pharmaceutical industry would be financially disastrous.

Tort reform is needed to halt out-of-control litigation before it prevents doctors from practicing effectively and according to evidence-based models and pharmaceutical companies from innovating. Proposals are being evaluated in several states and at the federal level. The proposals generally limit non-economic damages (commonly pain and suffering), to protect defendants, while not affecting actual damages, to protect plaintiffs.

The state of Mississippi passed tort reform into law in early 2003 that aims to curb frivolous lawsuits and establishes a sliding scale ceiling on punitive damages depending on the net worth of the defendant. This "reform" still has a way to go – non-economic damages can still be as high as $20 million – but it is a start.

One of the challenges facing us is the issue of paying for high quality evidence-based healthcare. Americans need to examine why we pay so much to receive so little. Are high-cost litigation and the practice of defensive medicine raising costs? Is a lack of true competition among health insurance plans raising costs? Should America increase governmental control of medical decisions? Should intellectual property law be changed? These questions need to be addressed without resorting to a system of price controls that will have the unintended side effect of squashing dynamic advancement.

The Global Picture

Healthcare's global tragedy is that treatable diseases afflict people in the poorest parts of the world. Approximately 40,000 children die every day from preventable conditions like diarrhea, malaria and measles – illnesses that have been all but eradicated from more developed areas. There exist preventions and cures for diseases that are not finding their way into the neediest populations.

Access to appropriate healthcare is not a charitable cause but a basic human right. Through partnerships with non-governmental organizations and other governments, industrial and technologically advanced countries can create sustainable, self-supporting healthcare systems and access to much needed medicines. Less developed nations deserve a voice in how that medicine is administered and to that end, organizations like the World Health Organization (WHO) and Doctors Without Borders can be instrumental in the dialogue. But while individuals and small organizations discuss the needs and potential solutions to these issues, and many wonderful groups are putting a dent in the problem, there has been little measurable impact on global public health. Developed nations should be looking for creative ways to support that dialogue and action and continue to strive for innovation.

But the inadequacies of developing nations' health systems must be addressed as a part of the equation. The Millennium Development Goals (MDGs), agreed to in 2000 by 189 countries of the United Nations, and supported by the International Monetary Fund (IMF), World Bank and other organizations, set one target as a two-thirds reduction in the mortality rate for children under five.

According to estimates, including those from the CDC, in developing nations, between 1.5 million and 2.5 million deaths each year in children under the age of five are attributed to diarrhea not associated with cholera. And forecasts indicate that child mortality in sub-Saharan Africa may not be reduced for another 160 years. With simple interventions like hand washing so difficult to implement in poor, rural settings, preventable illnesses will thrive.

Without the contributions of the pharmaceutical industry – in both development and delivery of new drugs – some of the most insidious illnesses could continue to run unchecked. According to WHO, there has been a significant reduction in the price of antiretroviral drugs offered to all sub-Saharan African countries, where infection rates are highest and inhabitants live below the poverty level. In some cases these reductions are more than 90 percent, reducing costs from about US$10,000 per year to as low as US$300 for some treatment combinations. It is this type of global collaboration that will improve quality of life and increase lifespan across borders.

A Place for Corporate Philosophy

There is a common sentiment – at big, midsize, and small companies alike – that this is an industry in which one can make a real difference to society.

PediaMed strives to raise the standard of pediatric medicine and care every day. To stay abreast of the changing needs of healthcare professionals and patients, the company encourages open dialogue and quick response to customer inquiries and requests.

These publics – the physicians, pharmacists, nurse practitioners, and physician assistants as well as managed care companies, HMOs and state Medicaid plans – are all stakeholders in the pharmaceutical industry, deserving of honest, value-added communications. Success is based on ensuring the value offered to all of those customers is of uniform high quality.

As our customers' expectations increase, we, in turn, have higher expectations of our employees, and we need to equip them with the development, training and support to respond better and faster. Pharmaceutical companies should ensure that everyone within the company is aligned with the company's vision, values and strategies, and communicate those values consistently and often. We are very focused on personal development, because a smart, hard-working employee who is committed to openness is essential to innovation and development.

Because doctors face an ever-increasing threat of potential malpractice suits, astute pharmaceutical companies must understand the hesitancy on their part to try something new regarding prescriptions. Add to that primary care office visits down to an average of six minutes per patient, and a burdensome patient-load being put upon physicians by the managed care system, doctors barely have the time to keep up with the latest research. A well-trained, well-intentioned sales force can supplement the physicians' knowledge of developments within the industry, on Capitol Hill and with the company's product offerings. Despite the added pressures, the fact remains, physicians appreciate a pharmaceutical company that understands all the demands they face and strives to help them do their job more effectively and efficiently.

A strong corporate culture is the foundation upon which you can do that. PediaMed has managed to foster a strong and positive culture, which ensures consistency of the end product. The people who represent the face of a company, those who interact with the healthcare professionals every day, are a reflection of the product being brought to market. It is one of those intangibles that adds value to a company. It's a topic of debate whether this quality is retained or destroyed when companies are acquired.

It is sometimes easy to be caught up in some of the more unsavory aspects of the political machinations of healthcare, but that is a challenge to overcome. Some people, depending on the organizational culture, get cynical and are bludgeoned into accepting mediocrity, rather than trying to rise above that and dream bigger. To counteract that, you have to have people aligned to a common vision and common goal. Improving and providing needed treatments to underserved patient populations is a daunting objective for a small company. Keeping a staff committed to that vision is surprisingly less difficult, because the objective is a noble and measurable one.

Final Thoughts

Just 100 years ago, Americans had half the average life span that they enjoy today, and many conditions that were once deadly or crippling are now easily treated. Parents no longer worry that their infants will die of diseases that felled tens of thousands years ago. The Centers for Disease Control and Prevention report that in 1900 there were about 48,000 cases of smallpox, including 1,500 deaths. Today smallpox has been greatly controlled to the point of near-elimination.

Former FDA commissioner, Mark McClellan, speaking before the First International Colloquium on Generic Medicine in 2003, pointed out that the reduction in mortality in the United States from cardiovascular disease alone has been valued at $1.5 trillion annually from 1970 to 1990. But despite the measurable strides of modern healthcare, the pharmaceutical industry faces ever-increasing negative public perception. The Pharmaceutical Research and Manufacturers of America (PhRMA), the industry association, is attempting to change this negative perception to highlight the contributions of pharmaceutical companies. They report that, in 2003, the industry as a whole invested an estimated $33.2 billion in discovering and developing new medicines.

These challenges can be parlayed into terrific opportunities, particularly for companies willing to stake out what they stand for as a corporation. Some of the most successful people in history have been able to align their ethics and their occupation to advance technology, improve the human condition and, at the same time, turn a healthy profit. Revenue and respect need not be mutually exclusive concepts to generate. It is possible to maintain a financially healthy company while fostering a genuine betterment of society, particularly when the end point is improved health and longevity. If specialty pharma sticks to doing one thing and doing it really well, the long-term rewards will be felt well into the future.

Dr. Cameron Durrant is President of PediaMed– The Pediatrics Company™, based in the greater Cincinnati area. He was formerly Vice President of Global Business Planning and Operations and Global Vice President of Infectious Diseases at Pharmacia Corporation (now Pfizer), based at Pharmacia World Headquarters in New Jersey. Prior to this position, he was with GlaxoSmithKline and Merck and Co.

He is a medically - trained MBA, and has worked as a medical practitioner in Australia and the UK. His medical experience included general medicine, geriatric medicine, general surgery, ENT surgery, pediatrics, obstetrics & gynecology, psychiatry, accident & emergency, primary care.

Cameron's extensive pharmaceutical experience encompasses directing global as well as local market launches, sales leadership, marketing and business management, US domestic and European P+L experience. He was honored by Med Ad News' Brand of the Year award.

He was also co-founder of a chain of private medical centers as well as a clothing business in Australia and founded the UK MBA Medics Group.

Dr. Durrant received his MBA from Henley Management College in 1995 and his MB and BCh from the Welsh National School of Medicine in Cardiff in 1983.

Dedication – To my family.

CEO Best Practices
Management & Leadership Strategies From 200+ C-Level Executives

This insider look at succeeding as a top executive is written by C-Level professionals (CEOs, CFOs, CTOs, CMOs) from the world's leading companies. Each executive shares their knowledge on how to get an edge in business, from leading a company to making money in a down economy to increasing your efficiencies in all areas of your business (marketing, financial, technology, hr, and more). Also covered are over 250 specific, proven innovative strategies and methodologies practiced by leading executives and CEOs that have helped them gain an edge. This report is designed to give you insight into the leading executives of the world, and assist you in developing additional ideas in all areas of your business that can help you be even more successful as a top executive.

WRITTEN BY C-LEVEL EXECUTIVES FROM COMPANIES AT:

Advanced Fibre Communications, American Express, American Standard Companies, AmeriVest Properties, AT Kearney, AT&T Wireless, Bank of America, Barclays, BDO Seidman, BearingPoint (Formerly KPMG Consulting), BEA Systems, Best Buy, BMC Software, Boeing, Booz-Allen Hamilton, Corning, Countrywide, Credit Suisse First Boston, Deutsche Bank, Drake Beam Morin, Duke Energy, Ernst & Young, FedEx, First Consulting Group, Ford Motor Co., Frost & Sullivan, General Electric, IBM, Interpublic Group, KPMG, LandAmerica, Mack-Cali Realty Corporation, Merrill Lynch, Micron Technology, Milliman & Robertson, Novell, Office Depot, On Semiconductor, Oxford Health, PeopleSoft, Perot Systems, Prudential, Salomon Smith Barney, Staples, Tellabs, The Coca-Cola Company, Unilever, Verizon, VoiceStream Wireless, Webster Financial Corporation, Weil, Gotshal & Manges, Yahoo!

$219.95

Call 1-866-Aspatore (277-2867) to Order Today!

Management Best Sellers

Visit Your Local Bookseller Today or www.Aspatore.com For More Information

- Corporate Ethics - Making Sure You are in Compliance With Ethics Policies; How to Update/Develop an Ethics Plan for Your Team - $17.95

- 10 Technologies Every Executive Should Know - Executive Summaries of the 10 Most Important Technologies Shaping the Economy - $17.95

- The Board of the 21st Century - Board Members From Wal-Mart, Philip Morris, & More on Avoiding Liabilities and Achieving Success in the Boardroom - $27.95

- Inside the Minds: Leading CEOs - CEOs from Office Max, Duke Energy & More on Management, Leadership & Profiting in Any Economy - $27.95

- Deal Teams - Roles and Motivations of Management Team Members, Investment Bankers, Professional Services Firms, Lawyers & More in Doing Deals (Partnerships, M&A, Equity Investments) - $27.95

- The Governance Game - What Every Board Member & Corporate Director Should Know About What Went Wrong in Corporate America & What New Responsibilities They Are Faced With - $24.95

- Smart Business Growth - Leading CEOs on 12 Ways to Increase Revenues & Profits for Your Team/Company - $27.95

Buy All 7 Titles Above &
Save 40% - Only $114.95

Call 1-866-Aspatore (277-2867) to Order

Other Best Sellers

Visit Your Local Bookseller Today or www.Aspatore.com For A Complete Title List

- Ninety-Six and Too Busy to Die - Life Beyond the Age of Dying - $24.95
- Technology Blueprints - Strategies for Optimizing and Aligning Technology Strategy & Business - $69.95
- The CEO's Guide to Information Availability - Why Keeping People & Information Connected is Every Leader's New Priority - $27.95
- Being There Without Going There - Managing Teams Across Time Zones, Locations and Corporate Boundaries - $24.95
- Profitable Customer Relationships - CEOs from Leading Software Companies on using Technology to Maxmize Acquisition, Retention & Loyalty - $27.95
- The Entrepreneurial Problem Solver - Leading CEOs on How to Think Like an Entrepreneur and Solve Any Problem for Your Team/Company - $27.95
- The Philanthropic Executive - Establishing a Charitable Plan for Individuals & Businesses - $27.95
- The Golf Course Locator for Business Professionals - Organized by Closest to Largest 500 Companies, Cities & Airports - $12.95
- Living Longer Working Stronger - 7 Steps to Capitalizing on Better Health - $14.95
- Business Travel Bible - Must Have Phone Numbers, Business Resources, Maps & Emergency Info - $19.95
- ExecRecs - Executive Recommendations for the Best Business Products & Services Professionals Use to Excel - $14.95

Call 1-866-Aspatore (277-2867) to Order